The Five-Card Pentagram Tarot

Tarot

**A Guide to Reading Your Tarot Cards
And the Five-Card Pentacle Layout**

By

Marv Machura

XXI - THE UNIVERSE

ISBN 978-1-09838-614-6

Images by Renata Lechner © 2019 Lo Scarabeo
All images used with permission

Edited and Cover Design by Alison Lund

For all seekers of truth, wisdom, and happiness!

**Dedicated to my parents and grandparents
who not only gave me life
but also showed me a way to live it
with respect, love, kindness, and joy.**

*You are a child of the universe
No less than the trees and the stars;
You have a right to be here.*

*And whether or not it is clear to you,
No doubt the universe is unfolding as it should.*

*Therefore be at peace with God,
Whatever you conceive Him to be.*

*And whatever your labors and aspirations,
In the noisy confusion of life,
Keep peace in your soul.*

*With all its sham, drudgery and broken dreams,
It is still a beautiful world.*

*Be cheerful.
Strive to be happy.*

- Max Ehrmann

Foreword

"Beauty is truth, truth beauty, —that is all
Ye know on earth, and all ye need to know."
- John Keats

I have often found that Tarot guidebooks are either too complex and multilayered or too simple and general. Thus, these guides either give the seeker too much information or not enough advice. With this guide, I have aimed to present a clear and focused interpretation of each card in the Tarot deck that provides the seeker with enough information to be useful and intriguing, but not too much information so that interpretations are overwhelming and perhaps not useful to the seeker.

In the interpretations that I provide for each card, I refer to the Universe as the supreme entity that it is. We are all children of the Universe. This is the starting and ending point for everything in this guide for the Tarot. If this book moves you into a closer relationship with the Universe, that would be wonderful.

I have been a teacher, performer, and writer, as well as a psychic over my career. I know that a lot of myself is in each interpretation of each card. As you read and work with this book you will get to know me. But I hope that this book allows you to get to know yourself more as well as love yourself more. I also hope that this book will expand your intellectual and spiritual life through that magical transformative process called learning. As you do this, I also consistency and significance in developing and practicing your own ritual and mediation as you enter into a reading and engagement with the Tarot.

Always treat the cards respectfully and store them in a safe and caring manner. As you engage in shuffling and drawing from each of the mini decks for your five-card layout, you should meditate on the mini deck's unique qualities and what you are asking of the Universe. For example, when you are about to draw from the Pentacles, you should meditate on earthly and material things; for the Cups, you should meditate on relationships and emotions. This guidebook provides further explanations of these qualities and offers sample meditations for each part of the Tarot that will comprise your five-card pentacle arrangement and related divination, advice, and fortune.

The following is one shuffling method you may use. Start by lightly knocking on the deck five times with your knuckle to clear the cards of their past energy and usage. Then cut the deck five times. For each of the odd cuts (1, 3, 5) cut the deck from the top; for each of the even cuts (2, 4), cut the deck from the middle leaving the top and bottom cards in place. After your fifth cut, draw whatever card is on the top of the deck. Place the card in its proper position in your pentacle. Do this with each mini deck in order, just as you would if you were drawing a pentagram with a pen in this prescribed order: Trumps, Wands, Cups, Swords, Pentacles. The number five is significant because there will be five cards in your layout matching the five suits of the Tarot aligning with the five points of a pentagram and pentacle.

This guidebook does not engage in interpreting upside down, or jumping cards (cards that slip out while shuffling.) If a card is drawn upside down, simply right the card back to its proper orientation and carry on. If a card falls out while shuffling, place it back in the deck and reshuffle.

The purpose of your five-card divination is to ask the Universe to give you timely advice, wisdom, and insight regarding your present situation and near future. It is done also to provide protection and good luck to you, the seeker. The pentacle and pentagram have long been used as protective and auspicious symbols or objects.

The word "pentagram" is differentiated from the word "pentacle" as follows. The word "pentagram" is mostly associated with the shape that is created when drawing a five-pointed star. The word "pentacle" is mostly associated with objects and mystical symbols that are in the shape of a pentagram with or without a circle enclosing the five points of the star.

There are two basic ways to engage in a five-card reading. One way is to draw one card and read its message and meaning. Then you move on to your second, third, fourth, and fifth card, reading each one prior to drawing the next card. Another way is to draw each of the five cards in succession, thus laying out your pentacle prior to engaging this guidebook. Once your cards are all drawn, then you can begin reading the meaning of each card. Both of these ways of laying out and reading your cards are equally good and depend only on your personal preference.

One thing to keep in mind is that all of the five cards you will draw are interrelated. This is to say, there are meanings to be found in parallel and diverse cards and in other aspects of how your pentagram completes itself. Unfortunately, this aspect of your reading is beyond the capacity of this book. This also illustrates another important point: a guidebook like this one, cannot replace a practicing psychic who works with the Tarot or other divinatory means. Psychic readers see into the cards by connecting with the vibrations of the seeker. Psychics are thus able to see the future as pictures in their minds.

Psychic ability exists in everyone, but only a few people have enough of this facility to engage in comprehensive or professional fortune telling and psychic counselling. Most people cannot see into the future and past as a practicing psychic can. Nevertheless, there are some guidelines that you can follow to better understand and interpret the holistic, five-card aspect of your reading.

After you have read each card's interpretation and as you look at your five-card pentacle, try to envision a way forward for yourself that brings all of your five cards together. Consider parallel cards (those with similar advice) as reinforcing each other. Consider that contrasting cards (those with diverse or opposite advice) are pointing to clashes within various elements of your life. For example, you may see contrasting cards from the Swords and Cups that indicate a conflict between your heart and mind. In the same way, contrasting cards from the Pentacles and Wands indicate a conflict between your energy and your resources. Sometimes the numbers of each card can be interpreted. For example, you can interpret a seven as being a stronger probability than a four. In a similar manner, you could see a Knight as being a stronger influence in your layout than a Prince.

Your five-card layout forms a special type of pentacle. As a pentacle, this layout gives you protection, support, and knowledge and all the good vibrations associated with this long-used symbol and shape. So when you look at your card layout, keep this in mind as you determine your way forward. The Tarot is never there to bring you down. It is there to uplift you and carry you onward to better things. When you combine the power of the Tarot with the power of the pentacle, as in your five-card layout, trust that the Universe is with you and wants what is best for you.

Be open and honest with yourself and trust that your life matters. You have freewill and much control over your life. You are an important part of the Universe. You are never alone. You cannot change the past and you cannot know everything about the future. But you have in each moment of your life a chance to learn, journey forward, love, laugh, cry, and live. Your life is not meant to be easy, painful, or predetermined; it is meant to be wondrous, multi-faceted, and purposeful. Never forget that it is *your* life, and perhaps the thing that matters most is to do the best you can with the great gift and miracle that your life is.

Here is a sample meditation for you as you begin your reading of the five-card pentacle layout. You can find other sample meditations given in the introductions to each of the five suits of the tarot in this guidebook.

Wonderful and life-giving Universe, help me at this given time; guide me on my journey and quest; give me timely advice that I need to hear so that I can best fulfil my purpose within the goodness and grace of the Universe for myself and others.

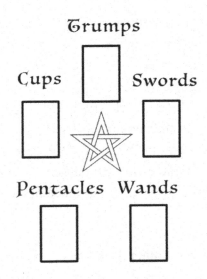

The Five-Card Pentacle Tarot Layout

Trumps

"What is a soul? It's like electricity—we don't
really know what it is, but it's a force that can light a room."
- Ray Charles

The Trump cards are the most important cards in the
Tarot and the most important card that you will draw for
your five-card layout. This Trump card gives advice for
your spirit and spiritual wellness. Your spirit is your entity,
your soul, your essence. Each Trump card represents a
particular aspect of the human spirit and there are 22 of
these cards in the Tarot. This card will rule over the other
cards that will complete your pentagram. As such, you
should give this card special importance in the five-card
reading.

If you are using another deck that is not the Millennium
Tarot, there will be some differences with the Trump cards.
The best way to deal with this is to use the numbers of the
Trump sequence to see equivalent interpretations for the
cards that are different from the ones that are presented here
and are part of the Millennium Tarot. For example, many
Tarot decks identify card XIV as "Temperance" rather than
"Art" as with the Millennium Tarot.

Keep in mind that your Trump card will give you
information on where your spirit will be heading in the near
future. The other four cards that you draw from the four
suits are important, but they should be read in context of the
general direction provided by your Trump card. This is to

say, your spirit is the most important thing to the Universe. Your money (Pentacles), your emotions (Cups), your mind (Swords), your strength (Wands) are all secondary to your spirit.

Practice a life that engages and amplifies your spirit; anything that diminishes your spirit needs to be eliminated from your life. Think of the other suits as giving you advice on how to do this with your money, emotions, mind, and strength. Trust and believe, beyond anything else, that the Universe is with you and wants what is best for you. The Universe does not want your spirit to be diminished, damaged, or worst of all, lost.

As with the other suits of the Tarot, you should meditate on the elemental meaning and properties of the suit from which you are about to draw before you draw the card from the Tarot.

Dear and Supreme Universe, where is my spirit at this time in my life? Please give me timely advice on where my spiritual journey will be heading in the near future. What is important for me to know and accept? Give me the strength and wisdom to use this knowledge for the betterment of both my own life and the lives of others.

0 The Fool

Risk - Fun - Adventure - Learning
Chance - Journey - Happiness - Growth

"Just keep taking chances and having fun."
- Garth Brooks

When you draw the Fool, your spirit will soon be adventurous, energized, and cheerful. Your spirit will want to step out of its ordinary routine and comfort zone, and you should listen to and follow this desire. These steps that you will take have good energy and the potential to dramatically alter the direction of your life in wholesome and exciting ways. So be confident that whatever you do will work out well for your spirit. As the first card in the Trump suit, the Fool can be seen as representing the primary step in the journey of your spirit toward enlightenment. In order to learn and grow, you need to take risks, get out there, and be ready for the transformations that are bound to happen.

Do something that your spirit has longed to do, but you have put it off due to mundane concerns and everyday excuses. Be more playful, carefree, and happy. Be daring and brave! In particular, do not be afraid of others calling you a fool or foolish. Embrace the foolishness in you. See the seriousness, intensity, and solemnity around you as ironically foolish. Let go of anything that has held you back from living a happier more engaging life; for example, you may have been holding a grudge or vendetta that has made your spirit the opposite of what this card represents.

Your spirit will dance, sing, and be happy. It is a beautiful world in spite of all its pretence, toil, and seeming imperfections. Do not sit around in a depressive, angry, or listless mood. As trite as this sounds, life is largely what you make of it. Realize and celebrate the fun and excitement of your life. You will not need to worry beyond basic safety and security where you are going and what you are doing. Do not hesitate to get started; take those first risky steps. Get out there! No excuses. Do things you love and love your life! Have fun! *Carpe Diem!*

I The Magus

Magic - Transformation - Positivity - Power
Excitement - Wisdom - Happiness - Growth

"There was a lot more to magic, as Harry Potter
quickly found out, than waving your wand
and saying a few funny words."
J.K. Rowling

When you draw the Magus, your spirit will soon be
confident, wise, and powerful. You will be nurturing and
exercising your intuitive and magical self. You have an
abundance of skills and abilities that are available for you to
use, and you should use them with power and authority to
benefit both yourself and others. Your spirit will be ready to

fly! Smile with self-assurance, authority, and respect for yourself. As you let the mysteries of the Universe swirl and sparkle around you, your spirit will become closer to the magical, transcendent, and transformational nature of the Universe. You will have the power to transform not only your own life but also the lives of others.

This card is telling you to aspire to the mysterious and metaphysical aspects of both life in general and your life in particular. You have keen powers, but do not take yourself too seriously. The monkey on this card should remind you of this crucial lesson in humility. Nevertheless, be confident of your magical power and be prepared to use it. You are golden, and all you touch with pure intention will be golden too.

Speak to all as equals, even if they are not, and use your gifts. You will bring joy and wonder to those around you and to your own life as well. You have much room in your spirit for many elements; this means that your open mind and humble spirit will want to experience and learn so much more. Continue to step into the light. Do not retreat into a cave. You are not a hermit. You are a magician. You need to be out there. *Abracadabra!*

II The High Priestess

Spirituality - Attraction - Strength - Vibrancy
Wisdom - Grace - Beauty - Power

"Nothing can dim the light that shines from within."
- Maya Angelou

When you draw the High Priestess, your spirit will soon to be in a breathtaking and powerful place, able to rise above the ordinary. Not only will you be moonstruck but others will be moonstruck by you. This will be a good thing as long as you do not indulge in this state of dazed wonder and euphoric longing. Keep your head in the stars but stay grounded. Close your eyes and feel life and learning within you glowing like the crystals pictured on this card. Cherish and continue to support this wonderful state!

Your spirit will be responsive, attractive, and ready to radiate outward. You should be encouraging, creative, and closer to the divine in all things and in all your relationships with others. You will be in a position to let good things come to you. As such, people are bound to be drawn to you and you do not need to pursue anyone or anything at this time. In addition, you will become a significant transformative force in their lives, and this will benefit you as well. Stay steady, confident, and true. Sparkle!

Do not use brute force to get through the conflicts in your near future. Instead, use a gentler, kinder approach that not only subdues your rational abilities and proclivities but also favours your intuition and passion. The more that you trust your clairvoyance, empathy, and powerful sensitivity, the better you will be able to use this time to its best advantage. Aim not only to keep your spirit under the spell of the High Priestess but also to learn from her as much as you can. Steer clear of those temptations and tempers that you know are contrary to your beautiful and wondrous essence. Shine on!

III The Empress

III - THE EMPRESS

Respect - Wealth - Strength - Generosity
Support - Responsibility - Grace - Nobility

"A life not lived for others is not a life."
- Mother Teresa

When you draw the Empress, your spirit will soon be in a respectable and powerful position. You will feel calm, generous, and nurturing. Many blessings will be coming your way, and you should be grateful. You will find that your spirit is ready to take on and be further strengthened by new responsibilities such as a new child or animal companion in your life. Regardless, expect your spirit to glow with all that you do for yourself and others. Your spirit will be in a regal, gracious, and important phase, and this wonderful period should continue into your future.

This will be a good time to use your wisdom, wealth, and power to help others, especially those close to you such as your friends and family. Your kindness and compassion will be needed. Also, consider joining and helping causes about which you feel passionate and personally involved. Your spirit will flourish even more when you involve yourself in the world in this way. For example, volunteering to work at a charity or non-profit for which you care deeply, such as the SPCA, will be not only wonderful for you but also great for the cause/organization of your choice.

You will be capable of handling this responsibility with wisdom, gentleness, and splendour. You will glow with a celestial green light as pictured on this card. This is a light that allows others to flourish and reach their potential. This will be a time to celebrate the divine aspects of your spirit and the spirit of the Empress with all her power and authority. You will be able to nurture those around you with the grace, knowledge, and kindness that you possess. You will be able to protect those needing your protection. As you embrace your power, beauty, and position, remember that kindness and compassion are signs of strength. Celebrate these qualities. All hail the Empress, the foundation and soul of any successful and wonderful empire, however big or small!

IV The Emperor

**Regality - Power - Influence - Calm
Rationality - Poise - Authority - Wisdom**

"Service to others is the rent you pay
for your room here on Earth."
- Mohamed Ali

When you draw the Emperor, your spirit will soon be in
a steady, noble, and powerful place. You will feel strong,
confident, and potent. You will feel that you have your life
in control. Your spirit will command respect and exert a
positive influence on others. You will be called upon to
arbitrate, judge, or otherwise decide upon weighty matters.
People will seek your counsel, or you will be in a position

that gives you no choice in the matter, such as being a parent, and you will *have* to rule. Be confident that you will rule wisely as you keep your own personal needs and wants in the background and focus on the greater good, the truth, and your clear moral sense of direction.

This card reassures you of your powerful identity, morality, confidence. You should not be looking to find yourself. Your sense of self will be resilient and able to take on all types of conflicts that may present themselves in your life. You should feel privileged to be in such a position rather than entitled. In addition, you should not feel that the burdens you have are weighing you down. Understand that with great power comes great responsibility. Direct your spirit and energy toward noble and good things in the Universe. Be just, fair, and principled. Maintain reserves of energy that are part of your deep underlying strength.

You will need to use your calm, rational, strong, and thoughtful nature. Trust that your heart is good, and do not do anything that your heart knows is wrong. Nevertheless, use your head and the tougher, realistic part of your spirit. This part of your spirit will be needed more than the softer, emotional part of your spirit. However, never harden your heart on your way to true, noble humanhood. Rule! Serve! You and your empire are bound for greatness, renown, and stability.

V The Hierophant

Wisdom - Confidence - Balance - Growth
Clout - Stability - Strength - Insight

"Great teachers touch the present,
preserve the past, and create the future."
- North American Proverb

When you draw the Hierophant, your spirit will soon be strong, poised, and true. You will feel a general comfort and confidence that comes to teachers and preachers after a lifetime of learning, practice, and certitude. Be confident that you can pass on wisdom to others for their benefit. You and your spirit will also benefit from this self-reliant, wise, and mystical place. Your spirit should remain in this happy state into the foreseeable future. You can carry the Hierophant as a key part of your being. This will be especially true if you maintain an open mind, a good heart, and engaging, productive work.

You will be concerned about those around you and their future. You will feel that you need to teach others what you have learned from life, and you should not hesitate to do this. In fact, there will be others who will be either directly or indirectly seeking instruction from you. Be careful, however, not to be too stern or disappointed when the lessons that you are trying to pass on seem to be ignored or unimplemented. There are no wasted words in the Universe, and your words of wisdom will carry on even if it appears that no one is listening. Also, recall that you cannot force people to change their minds; that is something they have to decide to do for themselves.

In your near future, do not bother with compromise and consultation. Also steer clear of anger and self-pity. You will make some mistakes along the way; you are only human, after all. But your faith in your abilities, your conviction in universal truths, and your confidence in the magical power of learning will continue to grow. Keep speaking your truth and teaching others all that you know. Keep the lamp of learning burning. Keep shining your light of truth on all things. Preach! Teach!

VI The Lovers

Intimacy - Love - Generosity - Enrichment
Growth - Completion - Energy - Transformation

"Life without love is like a tree without blossoms or fruit."
- Kahlil Gibran

When you draw the Lovers, your spirit will soon be experiencing the wonderful essence of love, intimacy, and togetherness with another person. This will transform your life and spirit in a good way, but you need to be ready for these changes to make the most of them. Although the most natural way to think of this card is in terms of a romantic union, it is not necessarily that way. There may be any number of ways that you will intertwine with another to create love, intimacy, joy, and wonder. Be open to them all. Do not let your spirit wander alone and lonely. But, do not rush or force this intimacy; it will happen in its own time.

Regardless of how your own circumstances suit this card, your spirit will bring new light and life into the world. This will be a happy and almost overwhelming time for you. A danger is that you may want to pull back and not assume so much responsibility. If you are single, you may want to remain single and alone. Or if you have a romantic partner, you may not want to make a deeper commitment with that person. Even if you are in a long-term marriage, you may not want to get closer to your partner. It is all risky! But it will be well worth the risk if you stay true, loving, open, and committed.

Your life will not become easier; it will become more difficult. But more difficult does not mean worse. You will be much richer, creative, fulfilled, and happy when this type of love enters your life and enriches your spirit. Here is the catch: be prepared for the depths of your sorrow to match the heights of your joy. Yet, do not be afraid and back away. You should be feeling lucky that you have been chosen for this wonderful moment and potential future. Stay true. Let go of the fear. Breathe deeply and commit to the wonderful union that is part of some divine plan that continues into the infinite and will now not end with just you, alone.

VII The Chariot

Protectiveness - Safety - Confrontation - Conflict -
Resolution - Victory - Strength - Vitality.

"Everybody has to fight to be free."
- Tom Petty

When you draw the Chariot, your spirit will soon be sensing that there are dangers and difficulties ahead; further, you will be feeling like the odds of success are not in your favour. You will feel threatened or discouraged by continual opposition and setbacks. In response to this, you may be wrongly indulging in self-pity asking that age-old question: "Why me?" You also may be questioning whether your beliefs, values, and purpose are worth hanging onto because so much of the world seems to be against you. Further, it is possible that you will sense that your personal safety is at risk due to events that have recently happened. Thus, your spirit will be in a defensive and protective mode.

Regardless of your situation, this card assures that you will be able to get through whatever opposition faces you with courage, strength, and stamina. Do not be afraid of direct confrontation. For example, face that bully at work or contact that neighbour who plays music too loudly. Let your protective armour as pictured on this card be temporarily put on. Once you have moved into the fight, done your best, and come out victorious, take off your helmet and let your hair blow freely in the wind! You are not meant to wear a real or metaphoric helmet all the time.

You will be facing outside threats, not internal ones. This will be especially true if people who are close to you, such as a lover, family members, or friends have battered or betrayed you. *It is not your fault.* Inside that tough shell and armour, you are soft and vulnerable, kind and caring, and afraid of emotional hurt much more than physical hurt. Hang on to your goodness, core values, and self-worth. They need protection always. Charge through! Ride it out! Do not despair. You will get through these battles.

VIII Adjustment

Suspension - Introspection - Adaptation - Positivity
Balance - Moderation - Correction - Respite

"Life is a balance of holding on and letting go."
- Rumi

When you draw Adjustment, your spirit will soon be experiencing a time of suspension and alteration. Your spirit will *not* be ready for you to go boldly forward or eagerly backward. You will need to draw inward for a time, suspend your actions, and listen to your inner voice. The truth and right path are out there: let your conscience be your spiritual guide. You may be needing any number of things, but the most likely thing will be moderation. This is to say that you will need to moderate some excess in which you are indulging. This can be anything from too much exercise to too much beer. Something will be putting your spirit off balance, and it is with this imbalance that you need to deal.

This card reminds you that everything will be okay as long as you are prepared to make some adjustment to your life. Ask yourself what do you need to hang onto and what do you need to let go to best travel forward. As mentioned above, ask yourself what excesses in your life need to be moderated. Moderation, a key to a well-lived life, will benefit your spirit now and long into your future. Moderation will lead to balance, and balance leads to spiritual wellness.

Be impartial as you look at yourself and your life. You are a complex mix of good, bad, light, and dark. You are not made to be simple and one dimensional. You will also need to strike a balance between blaming/crediting yourself and blaming/crediting others. Make the necessary adjustments and carry on with these *life* changes and be careful to not exchange one excess for another, such as excess beer for excess exercise. You *will* find that that beautiful balance that keeps your spirit healthy, humble, generous, loving, and kind.

IX The Hermit

**Transformation - Enlightenment - Insight - Education
Revelation - Prosperity - Truth - Goodness**

"The greatest satisfaction is not the decoration. It is
knowing that I am able to help someone who needs help."
- Jimmy Page

When you draw the Hermit, your spirit will soon
experience a divine revelation that will have profound and
wonderful effects for you and those around you. However,
you should keep this revelation of a higher truth to yourself
at first. The Universe will let you know when the time is
right and when those around you may be ready for deeper
insights into all things. Take time to wonder and wander

alone. Let your spirit be open to the beauty and miracle of life.

Your spirit will become much more interesting, more fertile, and more involved in life. You will feel as if you are walking out of the dark cave of your past life into the morning dawn and brilliant sunlight of a new day and new age. Everything will start looking different and, for lack of a better word, more real. Consider that a seed will be planted in your spirit that you will need to nurture. It is just a seed right now, as small as a sperm or ovum cell as pictured on this card. However, that microscopic cell contains enough information and potential to create the complexity of a fully-grown human being like yourself who can and will change the world.

Welcome this new sunrise. Do not go back into your cave. Hold your new inner treasure like a brilliant lantern that illuminates and blesses your path forward. You may consider that the Universe has rewarded your spiritual quest with a great jewel and selected you for some higher purpose. You will *sense* this change more than you can *know* or *understand* this change. Do not slip backward into your old ways. Do not be afraid of the way forward. Take time to listen, to think, to envision, to wonder. Above all, keep in mind throughout this time of *wandering*, that it is a *wonderful* life, especially with you, and your new awareness, in it.

X Fortune

Luck - Change - Anxiousness - Excitement
Action - Fate - Opportunity - Watershed

"Luck is when an opportunity comes along,
and you are prepared for it."
- Denzel Washington

When you draw Fortune, your spirit will soon be
experiencing changes. These changes, however, are not yet
clearly defined. When the wheel of fortune stops turning, it
will be pointing to something new, and hopefully something
good and exciting for you. Be thankful that the old is going
away, and the new is coming in. Although you cannot

control everything, you *do* have some control over this process, just as gamblers can control how much money they put on their bets. For your spirit, how you deal with the events forthcoming will be what counts. You have nearly complete control over this part of fortune. Your destiny is only 50% shaped by fate; the other 50% is how you deal with luck that comes your way.

You may have been stuck in something without even realizing it. The Universe wants to turn you out of that place into a better place. Let your spirit fill with excitement and adventure. There is a possibility of danger and sorrow ahead along with a possibility of joy and wonder. The point is to accept that something in your life will be changing, and it will be something over which you do not have control. Your life will soon settle into some new direction, and any anxiety and worries will fade as you engage in going forward with renewed vigor and stability.

Take time to carefully consider your actions and choices. They will be more important than usual. You will have the best possible fortune if you stay true to yourself. Although your fortune changes, it does not mean that *you* change. Also, remember that fortune smiles upon those who keep creating their own opportunities, those who do not give up, and those who do not despair. Trust the Universe, but also take matters into your own hands as much as possible. Look to the horizon! Place your bets! Give it your best!

XI Lust

Passion - Creativity - Energy - Danger
Risk - Transformation - Pleasure - Engagement

"Sex is a part of nature; I go along with nature."
- Marilyn Monroe

When you draw Lust, your spirit will soon be filled with creative energy and passion. It will be a potent vitality. You will find it difficult to contain or control. Trust that this dynamism is a natural and necessary part of your human condition. There is a reason for lust, just as there is a reason for all aspects of your humanity. Lust is a blazing hot fire, a ride in a fast car, and the roar of a lion. Lust drives you on, and you would not be here without this powerful element in the Universe. As such, recognize that lust is a key component in your both your mystical and physical journey on this planet. Climb on the lion's back as pictured on this card and enjoy the ride!

Keep in mind that lust is a force that can never be fully tamed and like all aspects of your spirit, lust has a negative side. So tread carefully but tread on. You should start an intense project, a passionate relationship, or any number of other things about which you will become impassioned. But be careful. Do not fall into the excesses that lust is prone to generate. Too much of anything is never good, but this is especially true with lust.

Do not be afraid to experience the powerful wonders of creation, take risks, and let go of the reins. Your life is not only about safety and security; too much of this equals a boring life for you. You should indulge in your creative zeal and let your spirit fill with cosmic drive and desire. You will be on a celestial ride with all its wonders, diversions, and purposes. Engage in the ardent fire of your being. Enjoy! Be grateful! Have fun! Ride on!

XII The Hanged Man

Pain - Misery - Sacrifice - Destiny
Suspension - Grief - Rebirth - Renewal

"As they say, when one door closes, another door opens.
But the hallways can be brutal."
- Dale Ripley

When you draw the Hanged Man, your spirit will soon be at a low point. Your spirit will feel suspended and not where you want to be. Be assured that your spirit is strong and that you will endure being the "Hanged Man" for a short time. Your spirit will be much stronger, happier, and advanced once you are able to carry on from this low point that you will soon be encountering. And, the sooner you accept that a current and important part of your life will be ending, the better it will be for you. Also accept that this will not be a pleasant ending: it is going to hurt. The good side is that you are about to be reborn into something better, something new. Do not lose hope in this time of darkness and transformation. As the saying goes "Hang in there."

The Universe is not punishing you. You will be a victim of some evil and misguided force over which you do not have control. In spite of all your sacrifices and efforts, there will be nothing you can do. Take some time to suffer and grieve. There is no strength without suffering. Although it may be hard for you to thank the Universe for this experience, giving thanks is something that you should and *will do*, eventually. Your life will be transcending your own existence in some way bringing positive change for you and others. These will be important and lasting changes.

As mentioned, resisting and fighting will only prolong the inevitable. Be the Hanged Man for a while; it is tolerable and necessary. You will soon be taken off the hanging tree and will be able to resume your life's journey toward some greater good. You will be tough enough to get through this. And once you come off the hanging tree, you will be even tougher. You will also be more advanced in your spiritual journey as divine transformation works its magic behind the scenes. Stay strong! The interim may be brutal. But all will be well and better than before.

XIII Death

**Abruptness - Finality - Distress - Pain
Shock - Sadness - Grace - Acceptance**

"The fear of death follows from the fear of life;
the person who lives fully is prepared to die at any time."
- Mark Twain

When you draw Death, your spirit will soon experience an abrupt and comprehensive transition. Something in your life will be ending suddenly and with the finality of death. This does not necessarily mean a life, or your life, will suddenly expire. But this card does mean that your spirit is about to feel this way, and overall, this will be a good thing for you and your spirit. Nothing lasts forever, and your spirit needs to be reminded of this to make the most of each moment of miracle that is your life.

This death (either real or metaphoric) will end something that needs to and is ready to end. This death will coincide with a birth because life and death are forever knit together in a sacred eternal circle. This card is also telling you to take time to contemplate your own death as well as the death of others in your life. As you do this, consider making some changes to your life while you still have it if there are things you that you would deeply regret once the final transition happens.

Everything in the mortal world will die, and there is nothing you can do about it. The only option with Death is to put it behind you as you carry on forward with your life. When you arrive at a point in your life when you are at peace with Death, accepting it whenever it comes, you will be in a very enviable position. This will be because you will be satisfied that you have given life your best and that you never gave up on life's mystical, spiritual essence. Continue to live life like you and others *are* going to die because you and others *will* die. Definitely not now, today, or tomorrow, but someday Death will come. All things pass.

XIV Art

**Creativity - Newness - Happiness - Satisfaction
Growth - Achievement - Alchemy - Bliss**

*"All children are artists; the problem is how to
remain artists once they grow up."*
- Pablo Picasso

When you draw Art, your spirit will soon be in a creative space able to combine elements and generate new things. Your spirit will be exposed to new ideas and receptive to new concepts and directions. You should not be afraid of failure, ridicule, or any other excuses that tend to stop people from engaging in the transformative power of artistic endeavour. If you are not already a professional artist, you should realize that art is not only for specialised artists; art and alchemy belong to everyone. The creation of any kind of art will have lasting and positive repercussions for your spirit.

This card is encouraging you to start, restart, or continue to engage your creative spirit. This could be something as simple as rearranging your home furniture in an innovative and creative way. It may be something more involved such as taking an art or photography course. It could be writing a journal entry in your long-neglected diary. There is nothing too simple or too complex for your spirit and its creative alchemic powers. You, as an artist, can transform anything you touch into something better than it originally was. This is as true for making a delicious meal from various ingredients as it is for carving a figure of a dog from a stick of wood. Creativity is creation.

Your life and spirit are creative, and this creative property is one of the most wonderful and joyous features of your humanity. Your life is not meant to be endured in drudgery. You need to sing, dance, and paint. Ignore the current attitude toward art that regulates it to the professionals and has the rest of us as passive consumers. It is never about fame with true art. Enjoy the mixology! Be creative. Be artistic. Exercise this wonderful alchemic power within you. Your hands and mind are meant for more than just work and passive entertainment.

XV The Devil

Confinement - Helplessness - Slavery - Deceit
Discouragement - Fear - Struggle - Addiction

"Recovery did not open the gates of Heaven for me;
it opened the gates of Hell and let me out."
- Unknown Author

When you draw the Devil, your spirit will soon be in a serious and potentially harmful situation. Your spirit would rather not be in this place. But instead of acting on your will, your spirit may be dangerously close to giving up since you will be seeing no possible way to change things. This is *not* good. And, it is *not* true! Your will has been tricked into believing that some outside force or Devil is in command of you. That is not, and can *never* be real. Only you are in command of you. The Devil's hands are tied as is pictured on this card. But this does not stop the Devil from making you hurt *yourself.*

This "Devil" will be present in your near future as either someone or something that will be causing ruin and distress in your life. You will need to identify and change this because it will not go away on its own. The first step will be to realize that you have the strength, intelligence, and freedom to make this change. Whatever this powerful thing is—and do not underestimate its power—let it go into your past. It will not be easy. But the alternative is to remain under its control: helpless and hopeless.

The healing power of hope, faith, and love will come back into your life. Your world will return to you as you regain your own power and freedom. You should make no more excuses and deals with the Devil. You should make a deal with yourself. Do not give yourself over to those misguided and destructive powers that want to control your life and deprive your soul of joy, wonder, and freely chosen identity. Be yourself. Love yourself. Love life. Do not give up! You are born free. Aim to die free as well.

XVI The Tower

Catastrophe - Endings - Destruction - Ruin
Wreckage - Waste - Devastation - Annihilation

"New and wonderful beginnings are often
disguised as painful endings."
- Lao Tzu

When you draw the Tower, your spirit will be about to
undergo dramatic and catastrophic changes. Unfortunately,
there will be not much that you can do about it. The process
may have already started, or your spirit may be able to see
or sense it coming. Whatever reasons why will not matter.
The forces will be too strong to resist. You will close a

chapter of your life and will soon step forward into a new one. This part of your life's journey will make you stronger, more resilient, and happier.

Consider making a home renovation decision. Sometimes the best way forward with the renovation is a total demolition of the old building, so that you can start more-or-less completely new, rather than trying to save the old building. Think about all the work and investment that would be required to renovate an old, rundown house versus the work and investment in purchasing a new home. This card is telling you to go with the new home. Whatever it may be, the best way forward for your spirit will be a complete and unreturnable break with the past.

This impending demolition of the old and starting anew can apply to relationships, careers, possessions, or other things that have gone too far to repair. In this process you will need to be careful to not fall into the traps of paralyzing self-pity, useless anger, or pointless aggression. It will be okay to be sad and angry, but it will not be okay *to stay* sad and angry. It is better to walk away from a falling down building than remain inside trying to hold it up. It is better to be *from* a broken home than to live in one. All towers tumble. Move on. Let go. Start anew. It will not be easy, but it will be well worth it for you and your spirit. You have a lot more living to do! Do not look back.

XVII The Star

Enlightenment - Love - Beauty - Health
Mystery - Wonder - Growth - Radiance

"I am happy and being happy keeps you looking young."
- Olivia Newton John

When you draw the Star, your spirit will soon undergo a pronounced blessing that will be many faceted and as such, affect your life in many positive ways. Remain open to all these wonderful possibilities. Let them shimmer and shine in your life. Your spirit will be full of starlight and wondrous creative energy, and these blessings can continue for a long time into your future, especially if you keep nurturing these beautiful parts of your spirit and your life.

This card is encouraging you to detach your spirit from the everyday material world of work and worry and let mystery, wonder, and divine inspiration enter. You will be able to use this soul force to bring even greater blessings into existence for both you and others. Your spirit will be growing and glowing like the magnificent crystals that are pictured on this card. Do not be afraid of taking on new responsibilities and in helping others with your bright spirit. Be the star. Your shining spirit will restore hope and faith to others whose hope and faith have sadly withered.

You should surround yourself with beautiful, bright, and shining things in material form and in metaphysical forms of thought and action. Further, you should be open to divine inspiration and personal communion with the beauty and wonder of the Universe. You will say goodbye to any self-loathing, self-pity, and other destructive tendencies. This will have nothing to do with deserving. This will have everything to do with just being yourself, as well as being receptive to the mystery, beauty, and wonder within and around you. Stay humble, grateful, happy, and willing to share your spiritual and physical gifts with others. You are a wish come true. You *are* a star!

XVIII The Moon

XVIII - THE MOON

Uncertainty - Danger - Risk - Change
Happiness - Fun - Mystery - Excitement

"It is okay to let yourself go, as long
as you can get yourself back."
- Mick Jagger

When you draw the Moon, your spirit will soon be in a
transformational phase. These changes will be very
mysterious and potentially frightening, but if all goes well,
your moonlight transformations will be wonderful, and you
will come out of this phase stronger, less fearful, happier,
and more in tune with the mysterious and profound aspects

of your spirit. Also, your spirit will develop a closer relationship with the Universe. You should not be afraid, or at the very least, you should not let fear stop you from living a full, complete, and exciting life.

This card is encouraging you to step into the night, both physically and metaphysically. It will be a time for you to celebrate the moon's mystery, influence, and wonder. In this you may feel like the ocean tides that swell and recede via the immense gravitational power of the moon. And while this loss of control can be worrisome, it will be necessary. The night is not always a time for sleep. It is a time for nighttime fun, mystical experience, and romance. You cannot always be in the sun. Your spirit needs the moonlight too.

Nevertheless, do not go too far; be sure that you can bring yourself back. In all of this there will be a real danger of becoming stuck in the darkness, ever pulled and pushed by the tides of life, and not being in control of your life. Nevertheless, do not let the fear of the unknown stop you from falling in love, following your dreams, and making new friends. In the darkness, the moon reflects the life-giving sun, reminding you that the sun continues to shine always. So make your nighttime, moonlight revelries reaffirm the beautiful light of the day that is to come. Let your dancing in the moonlight reflect and affirm your joy of living life to the fullest and not be a rejection of your daytime responsibilities.

XIX The Sun

XIX - THE SUN

New Life - Light - Direction - Certainty
Happiness - Growth- Laughter - Joy

"The purpose of life is to be happy."
- The Dalai Lama

When you draw the Sun, your spirit will soon be full of sunlight and joy. This will be a doubly happy time for you because you are the one largely responsible for this cheerful state of your spirit. This type of spiritual bliss is not an accident. It is the real deal. Hopefully this wonderful state will continue long into your future. Life is complex and continues to evolve. So treasure these seemingly endless sunny days coming your way. In times like these, gratitude can and will continue to enhance your life, prolong the bliss, and encourage more moments of joy and wonder.

Your spirit will be in a period of remarkable transition. You may be bringing new and wonderful life into the world both physically and metaphysically. For example, you may be conceiving a child, getting married, writing a book, or growing a garden. The point is that you will be doing all these things for the right reasons, and as such, these things are bound to enrich your spirit as well as others. Do not be afraid of the light or the changes and growth that the light brings; otherwise, these moments and opportunities may slip past you.

There is nothing that you can comprehend and experience in your daily life more vivid and powerful than the sun. Consider that you can be like the sun in your life and the lives of others. You have the power to change any day from dark and gloomy to light and bright. This card is encouraging you to practice and celebrate this power. Also, keep in mind that the cultivated memory of these sunny, blissful days will help you overcome the melancholy that is bound to recur in your life. The sun cannot shine every day, so store these precious moments. These memories will chase away the darkness when shadows inevitably fall and threaten your spirit. Let *your* light shine! Be happy.

XX The Aeon

XX - THE AEON

Change - Wonder - Mystery - Renewal
Excitement - Energy - Rebirth - Joy

"Just when the caterpillar thought life
was over, it became a butterfly."
- Unknown Author

When you draw the Aeon, your spirit will soon be at a significant transitional point in your life. You will feel that one age or aeon is ending and a new age is beginning. This large-scale change will be bringing you good fortune as well as positive spiritual growth. This type of complete spiritual and physical transformation will happen over many years.

As such, it will only be in hindsight that you will be able to settle on a date or event that marks the start of your new age or aeon. You will be at one of these marking dates or events in your life, whether you are aware of it or not.

One of the most important choices that you make each day is how you are going to act, react, and feel in any given moment. Sometimes, such as in your near future, your old world burns down and a new one rises up from the ashes. Your response to this event is what counts. This card is encouraging you to respond with gratitude, excitement, and hope. Spread your golden wings and take flight as pictured on this card. Make a conscious choice to make the best of whatever it is that lies ahead. Pursue happiness, meaning, and purpose.

There will be good times ahead for your spirit if you remain open to trying new things, meeting new people, and entertaining new ideas. Who knows where it may lead? Time will tell. For example, something as simple as adopting a stray kitten from the SPCA can create a whole new world for you. It will be okay for you not knowing how or when your new aeon begins. Stay curious, hopeful, and open-minded as you continue the epic, mysterious, and wonderful journey that is your life.

XXI The Universe

Contentment - Ecstasy - Cheerfulness - Wisdom
Insight - Fulfilment - Friendship/Family - Love

"Life is not a process of finding yourself;
it is a process of creating yourself."
- George Bernard Shaw

When you draw the Universe, your spirit will soon be
fulfilled, creative, and happy. You will feel like you are on
the glorious summit of a mountain that you have climbed.
You will have had many hardships and will have spent
much effort to get to this place of spiritual bliss. Be affirmed
that you should continue with the path and direction of your

life that your spirit has been travelling. Use this time to advance your spirit to even higher levels of wisdom, contentment, and joy.

You will be engaged in creative, challenging, and fulfilling work and activity. If your spirit has been suffering any type of sadness related health or wealth, be assured that this suffering will be going away. And further, be assured that your suffering will be replaced by joy and satisfaction. You will feel very grateful, blessed, and happy. You will better understand that you cannot know what happiness is unless you also know what sadness is. Further, and importantly, you will understand what the Dalai Lama means when he says, "Happiness is not something ready-made; it comes from our own actions."

This is not to say that there will be no more spiritual issues in your upcoming life, but for now, you will find the kind of peace and happiness that comes from certitude, faith, and awareness of your place and purpose in the Universe. Let your spirit feel the all-encompassing love that comes from family, friends, and colleagues. Share your love with others as well. In this way, your own love will continue to grow. Does it get any better than to feel intimately connected with the Universe? Is there anything higher than helping the Universe move and turn in harmony, grace, and love?

Wands

"Live a long, long time before you get old."
- Ian Tyson

After you have drawn and placed your Trump card at the top of your pentacle layout, the next card to draw is from the suit of Wands. This card is placed at the bottom right of the pentacle layout.

The suit of Wands is associated with the element fire. Fire is the element that relates to your energy, strength, life force, and physical disposition such as feeling lazy, powerful, or motivated. The card that you draw from the Wands will provide you with timely advice regarding these aspects of your life.

The words "energy" and "fire" are closely related to the word "spirit." We often use the word "spirit" to refer to our energy and attitude; for example, "I am in good *spirits* today." As a result, there may be some confusion differentiating Trumps and Wands. If and when the word "spirit" is used in conjunction with Wands, it means life force and physical/mental energy. Wands are not referring to the word "spirit" as your essence or your soul.

In the Universe everything is related and connected to everything else. Therefore, as you read your card from the Wands, its message will be intertwined with the other cards that you will draw to form your pentacle layout. As mentioned in the introduction, reading the relationships between the cards is not part of this guide, but there are some rules that you can follow. See pages 17-18.

If you are not using the Millennium Thoth deck, you may find some differences with the cards. For example, Ryder-Waite Tarot decks go from Ace to 10, Page, Knight, Queen, King. The Millennium Thoth deck goes from Ace to 10, Princess, Prince, Queen, Knight. You will have to correspond these cards to their given sequence when engaging in a reading.

As mentioned, the suit of Wands gives you timely advice regarding your energy and strength. You need energy and vitality to have a purposeful and meaningful life. You are not meant to be a passive, listless, or apathetic observer. You are meant to engage in the magical song and dance that is your life.

You are built for action, reaction, conflict, and struggle. Without conflict, you have no story. Without struggle, you have no strength. Without action, you have no manifested will. Thus, pay close attention to what Wands represent for you. It is not an accident that this is the first card that you draw from the Tarot suits. You need to treasure and nurture your life force because without it, there is not much that you can or will do. So light that fire of yours and consult the Tarot how to best keep it burning brightly!

Divine spirit of fire, let me know how I can best apply my vitality and life force at this time in my life. What do I need to know to about my energy and strength to carry forward for the betterment of both myself and others?

Ace of Wands

Authority - Meaning - Purpose - Independence
Engagement - Initiative - Success - Reward

"The way to get started is to stop talking and begin doing."
- Walt Disney

When you draw the Ace of Wands, you will soon have more than enough fire and energy in your life. Dive in and get to work manifesting your will. You will be blessed with good vibrations. Do not waste your time on useless pursuits and passive activities such as watching too much television. Start something new or continue with a project that you have already started with renewed energy and enthusiasm. Your hands and mind are made for work and creativity. They should not be idle; they need to be put to use. Your happiness and much more depend on it. Although you may often dream of a life of unlimited leisure and pleasure, you would not be happy in that life. You need to engage in something purposeful, meaningful, and challenging.

Nevertheless, do not overload yourself with too many different jobs or projects at this time. This card recommends that you focus on one main thing. You should give this important aspiration, activity, or project your full attention, your steely determination, and your positive energy. As you do this, you will be successful. Your success will also help others. As long as you keep going forward manifesting your goals and aspirations, your energy and life force will continue to burn brightly. As an old English proverb goes, "Nothing succeeds like success."

When your passion is involved, there is no need for external motivation. So look inward, not outward for your solutions and enthusiasm. You will keep yourself healthy and happy as you take responsibility for these and other aspects of your wellness and energy. You will say good things about your body and mind, and you will stay in control of your life and your forward progress. You should imagine that you are the captain of a beautiful ship that is ready to set sail on the magnificent voyage that is your life. Take the helm and lean into the wind! Once you are underway, keep going through the rough waters that are bound to confront you and when your personal energy burns low. Ultimately enjoy the ride toward your destination. Steady as she goes. Engage!

Two of Wands

Confidence - Strength - Goodness - Energy
Productivity - Potential - Empowerment - Advancement

"We often become who we believe ourselves to be."
- Mahatma Gandhi

When you draw the Two of Wands, you will soon be filled with confident energy and power. You will believe in yourself and your personal expertise. This positivity will allow you to make big strides forward with your life. If you have been having doubts and negative thoughts about yourself, you will find a way to end those thoughts and return your inner voice to positive affirmations. As Bruce Lee has said, "Do not speak negatively about yourself, even in a joke." Also keep in mind the ancient wisdom that words cast spells; this is why it is called "spelling."

Consider that you are up to bat in a baseball game. When you swing the bat, you need to believe that you *will* hit the ball. This confidence is as important as anything else that you do in preparation for the game. This confidence applies to all other skills such as playing an instrument, singing a song, or giving a speech. When you believe in yourself, your energy is unstoppable. You will experience this type of confidence. So stop the monkey chatter in your brain that can and will give you doubts and fears. Belief is extremely powerful and so is the loss of faith. When you lose faith, it sucks the energy out of you as fast as air leaves a punctured tire. The result for you is the same as for the car, no forward motion. So practice and live your faith each day so that it grows stronger.

Take on a can-do attitude, not comparing or contrasting yourself with others. You should step forward with confidence, determination, and a positive self-image. To continue with the baseball analogy, you may not hit the ball every time you go up to bat, but you must believe that you will hit the ball every time you go up to bat. What is the alternative? Either never going up to bat or believing that you will strike out each time. Neither option is for you. As Henry Ford said, "If you believe you can't, you're right." You will have confidence. You will have energy. You *are* capable of great things! Step up to the plate, stare down the pitcher, dig in your cleats, raise the bat, believe! *Never* stop believing.

Three of Wands

Energy - Positivity - Teamwork - Cooperation
Celebration - Progress - Advancement - Reward.

"I get by with a little help from my friends."
- John Lennon, Paul McCartney

When you draw the Three of Wands, your energy will be stable, strong, and joyful. You will be going forward with new ventures or expanding existing ones. You will have the fire to take centre stage. Your light will shine and provide a positive and stable influence not only for you but also for those around you. This will be a time to seize opportunities that are offered to you. Do not let negativity and worry tie or slow you down. Realize that your energy will burn brighter when in use, especially now. So, use it or risk losing it. Your future and your fire will both be bright.

Gather others around you who can assist you in your projects, dreams, and aspirations. Together you will have more power and related success that flows from the combined energy and communal fire of a closely-knit team. However, do *not* let too many people in. The Three of Wands points to keeping your team small, perhaps no more than three people. You will soon be having a good time celebrating your common values, mission, and goals. These gatherings will make wonderful memories.

Although you will be doing so well and attainting so much, stay humble and grateful for all with which the

Universe has blessed you. As mentioned, you and your team will be successful, but as you congratulate yourselves and celebrate, be sure that your self-congratulations are brief and serve to reaffirm your values and mission. After a short rest and recharge, you and your team should get back in the game with renewed purpose, direction, and fire. Ready, set, go! Game on.

Four of Wands

Energy - Enthusiasm - Teamwork - Encouragement
Progress - Celebration - Support - Advancement

"No matter how smart you are,
you need a good team to build an empire."
- Steve Jobs

When you draw the Four of Wands, your energy and fire will soon be strong and stable. You will be seeing many happy outcomes stemming from this dynamism and drive. You will feel supported by those around you, and they will assist and encourage you. They will be able to lift you out of any depression or lethargy that you may be feeling; indeed, they will be capable of giving you the boost you need. Keep your mind and your schedule open to this possibility. This type of external encouragement and inspiration can come from unexpected sources and at unexpected times.

You should surround yourself with others who will help stoke your fire. Your personal fire and energy can be put it out by others who do the opposite. So steer clear of people who bring you down and take away your energy and passion for life. If there are any people who have been diminishing your enthusiasm, move them out of your life, or find some other way to reverse or eliminate their negative influence. You will be feeling great when you are able to move on from certain memories that have bothered you, and in particular, those memories that can act as energy sinks such as when someone once told you that you were no good at doing something.

You will be living the proverb that *you cannot do everything on your own*. There is a cooperative aspect to your life, and you will need to honour and cultivate relationships with those who have helped and will continue to be with you as you go forward. Your friends will stay close to you as you consult and discuss with them. And this teamwork will be even more effective when you take time to celebrate, not letting your life get so focused or busy that you forgo these good times with those important people in your life. The wheels are turning, and you and your team are going places. You will get there in time, so enjoy your journey as well as the company of those who support and encourage you along your way. All together now! Cheers!

Five of Wands

Depression - Stress - Stagnation - Negativity
Listlessness - Apathy - Dejection - Slump

"Life begins on the other side of despair."
- John-Paul Sartre

When you draw the Five of Wands, there will soon be something wrong with your energy and fire. You will need to stop and figure this out before you are able to move forward. You will feel depression, hopelessness, and disappointment. These negative emotions can create a barricade that saps your health and vitality. You will not be able to regain your health and energy until you overcome whatever negative forces are causing you to lose hope in your future.

Your body's general health and fitness are the first guard posts against depression and hopelessness, so do what you can to maintain and upgrade your fitness in spite of your despondency. You will also need to assess and alter the negative energy fields that are root causes of your stress. These negative energy fields are generated by certain types of people, jobs, and places. You can sense these negative vibrations, and these feelings will be accurately telling you what needs to change. You may have been taking medications to deal with your problems, and if so, that is okay, as long as you realize that medications only alleviate the symptoms of these types of afflictions. They are not a cure. For example, if your job is bringing you to a state of hopelessness, despair, and exhaustion, it is your job that needs to change, not your medication.

Although you will be thinking that life is awful, hopeless, and miserable, it is not that way. The worst possible outcome will be for you to lose your faith and hope, wallowing in self-pity and paralyzing despondency. As you picture a better future for yourself, decide to do one thing differently or decide to stop one thing that you know is causing your problems. Start slowly, if necessary, sustaining one or two of these positive changes. This will help you regain your proactive energy. You will see that it is really all about you and that you do not need to look to or blame others. Consider why should you seek outside help if you feel truly helpless? Without hope, there is no energy, no health, no point. So do not feel helpless; the Universe will always be there to help, and it blesses those who help themselves. Fix your fire.

Six of Wands

Overextension - Exhaustion - Frustration - Fatigue
Imbalance - Unproductivity - Disparity - Blockage

"Long-term consistency trumps short-term intensity."
- Bruce Lee

When you draw the Six of Wands, you will soon be in a place where you will need to be careful with your energy or fire because it will be in danger of losing its vigor and going out. You will have been putting your energy into too many things at the same time. As a result, you will be near exhaustion. You will feel unfocused and unmotivated. You will be suffering the effects of not maintaining a good balance between charging forward and recharging. This card is not full of foreboding; this is a gentle warning about your future. All will be well, and you will feel reenergized and refocused with a return to more conservative, stable, and moderate ways. Aim for a balance between rest and activity.

You should focus on your long-term goals as if you are running a marathon rather than a hundred-yard dash. You will be stronger and achieve more this way than you will in a frantic expenditure of your energy chasing your short-term goals. Another way to think of this is that you should not be spreading yourself too thinly. You cannot do it all, and do it all well. This will be a good time for you to reassess what is best for your spirit and your happiness. Step outside of the capitalistic race that you have been running, always hurrying, with some vague idea of arriving at a better place at some elusive point in the future. Focus on the present. Live in the moment.

While there will be times when you need to sprint ahead and start new projects and challenges, this will not be that time. You will need to get back to basics. You will need to put a hold on or end unnecessary and overly-stressful aspects of your life. At the very least, you will need to pace yourself in what you have begun and that with which are currently engaged. You have a long journey ahead of you. So take a deep breath and a timeout. Regroup and keep it together. You are in a good place and on the right path. Make the necessary adjustments for the long road ahead. Slow and steady *will* win this race.

Seven of Wands

Trials - Troubles - Conflict - Temptation
Challenge - Difficulty - Struggle - Obstruction

"The tallest oak in the forest was once
just a little nut that held its ground."
- North American Proverb

When you draw the Seven of Wands, your energy will
soon be required to lock onto your course, stand your
ground, and meet challenges that will be forthcoming. Your
strength and energy will be tested. But you will prevail. You
have the necessary vitality and power to overcome all
obstacles in your path. Trust yourself. You are much
stronger than you think you are. Do not let the conflicts and
complications that will be forthcoming change you in any
negative way. Accept them and deal with them. As you do
this, you will become stronger. Recall the old saying "No
struggle, no strength."

Do not compromise your goals and your ideals. There
are times when compromise is the best way forward, but
there are other times, such as the times ahead, when you
need to stand firm in your convictions. You are coming
from a place of strength, so do not listen to those who may
try to trick you into some form of surrender. Stay confident.
Do not concede, give in, or give up. Feel energized and
encouraged. You *will* be tempted to give up or avoid the
conflicts. For example, if you have a large amount of work
to do, you may find reasons to delay starting it. If you have

to confront a bully, boss, or co-worker, you may find excuses to not engage with this person. Sometimes in these types of cases, you will overindulge in food, drugs, and alcohol as a means of escape from the responsibilities you face. Sometimes you may lash out at good people as a consequence of not facing your real enemies and opponents. Be wary of these temptations.

Lock your sights on your way forward toward your goals and let your strength deal with any negativity that comes your way. It is a good idea, as well, to study your opposition or enemies to see how they can best be defeated or avoided. Take a look, also, at your own weak spots and reinforce them. You cannot be too prepared. All is going to be fine; nevertheless, be ready for opposition and trial. Keep reserves of your energy and your fire ready to go. Keep marching. Keep singing *your* song. Stand on guard. Do not back down. Your enemies will surrender and retreat, not you.

Eight of Wands

Anger - Frustration - Harm - Danger
Impetuosity - Temper - Obliteration - Rage

"If you are patient in one moment of anger,
you will save 100 days of sorrow."
- Chinese Proverb

When you draw the Eight of Wands, you will soon be having serious difficulty with your fiery energy. In fact, you will have the potential to explode with rage smashing everything around you into pieces, literally or metaphorically. Of course, this is not what you want to do. This card is warning you of this and encouraging you to make some changes that can stop this potentially dramatic and harmful situation from happening and interfering badly in your life. Your temper will need to cool down. You will need to be patient. You will get through this on your own, and it is not necessary to lash out in rage. You will be victorious, or you will fail. But you certainly *will lose* if you "lose it."

You will be feeling as if you are stuck in a rut and have been spinning your wheels without making any forward progress. In your frustration, you may feel like stomping on the gas pedal in anger and bad temper while your tires burn in the frictional heat of that furrow or pothole. But your madly racing engine will not remove your car from the rut. It will be time for a different approach. If you need a tow truck, make the call. In other words, do not make your situation worse than it has to be by expending your energy (and your car's engine and tires) in pointless, destructive, and dangerous ways.

Blistering, anger-driven energy will be your worst adversary in times like these. Perhaps the Universe put you into this metaphorical or real rut to save you from some type of more serious damage that would have happened if you had just kept speeding ahead on that slippery mountain road. All things happen for a reason. Trust the bigger picture; stop hurting yourself and blowing up at others. Do not harm yourself by thinking everything is against you because that is not true. Practice patience and acceptance. Feel the real strength that comes from these two key virtues in your life and your future.

Nine of Wands

Overwork - Overextension - Exhaustion - Collapse
Staleness - Decline - Imbalance - Unproductivity

"Take rest: a field that has rested,
produces a bountiful crop."
- Ovid

When you draw the Nine of Wands, you will soon need to pause and take a close look at how your energy is being managed in your life. Afterward, you will need to make some adjustments to better balance your life and its energies. There will be problems ahead for you if you do *not* make changes. You have been doing too much and succeeding at most of it, but you need to balance your activity with rest and reflection. You do not have much to worry over. You are not in a mess that needs to be cleaned up; if anything, you are too structured and organized, and thus, you need to have a bit more messiness in your life. You are not a machine, so do not treat yourself like one.

For your light to shine brightest during the day, your light requires the rest and the darkness of night. You need to recharge those batteries that make your light shine. Get more sleep. Get more recreation. The word "recreation" literally means re-*creation*. You need recreational time in your life to keep your creative energies flowing. You will get more, and better, work done when your life is balanced with work, rest, and recreation. Stop convincing yourself that there will be a day in the uncertain future when you can take a break from your frantic pace. You will need that break now, and you will always need these types of breaks. As such, it is a good idea for you to start adhering to a regular routine of yoga or some other recreation. Schedule it in your day planner and make time for it.

Keep yourself centered and composed. Realize that you are coming from a position of strength. It is important to note that this strength has come from the struggles in your past. You have overcome many arduous conflicts with deliberate action and steady progress. Keep this in mind as you travel forward; success is practically assured at this point in your life, especially if you follow this card's advice. Do not burn out. Regain your passionate fire. Remove the imbalance from your life. Take that much needed rest stop on your journey. Get outside. Breathe. Stretch. Recenter yourself. Life is good! And it is even better after a good night's sleep!

Ten of Wands

Retreat - Defeat - Blockage - Barrier
Detour - Redirection - Boundary - Endings

"A good retreat is better than a poor fight."
- Irish Proverb

When you draw the Ten of Wands, you will soon need to be both careful and defensive with your energy and life force. You will need to pull back from something for which you have been striving. Whatever it may be, you will need to either take a long pause in your pursuit or give up your endeavour completely. Sometimes in life, you have to know when to let go and when to hold on. You will know what to do if you trust your intuition and engage in honest self-assessment. While there are times when stubbornness and tenacity are best, this will not be one of those times.

Sometimes there are things that you would like to achieve, but they are unobtainable. Often these unattainable things are not advancing your truer goals or those things that are closer to your spirit and purpose. Are your ambitions and aims coming from other places than yourself and your own will? Are you being pushed into a wrong direction by parental or societal pressure, unnecessary competition, or revenge motivations? Expending your energy going after these things will be a tragic waste for you. You will need to reconnect with your spirit and redirect your life, advancing on your *own* journey with more happiness and joy. You *are* capable of doing great things, and these things will happen as you aim your life forward with practicality, honesty, and feasibility.

Imagine that you are walking along a path and have come upon a locked gate as pictured on this card. What do you do? You should not give up. You should not waste your time and energy in futile struggles against the gate. The best thing to do is to turn around and regroup. You will soon find another path with open gates. Maybe on this forced detour you will find something incredible and life altering. Regardless, the main thing is to gracefully and maturely accept this blockage. In spite of what the pop psychologists and motivational speakers may say, not everything is possible in the Universe. There are always limits. There are always locked gates. There are also signs that say do not enter, danger ahead. This will be one of those times for you. Beware. Be careful. Be smart. Be flexible and adaptable. This is a sign of strength and wisdom, not weakness and failure.

Princess of Wands

Energy - Passion - Purpose - Direction
Confidence - Power - Intensity - Success

"When you have a dream, you've got
to grab it and never let go."
- Carol Burnett

When you draw the Princess of Wands, you will soon not only be stepping forward in your life with purpose and energy, but also stepping forward with gusto, grace, and beauty. You will be feeling like you are walking on air! You will have young, vital energy, regardless of your age. Whatever is giving you this boost and passion needs to be identified, cultivated, and treasured. It may be some cause about which you are passionate, but it may also be a business idea, a new job, relationship, or any number of things that have you fired up. All good! Let your passion and energy burn.

Be prepared to feel like there is something crazy and uncontrollable about your fiery life force. Do not fight this. Accept it; enjoy it! It is a great blessing, so treasure these feelings and these times. This type of burning, joyful energy and forward progress cannot be sustained in the long term. Nevertheless, you can work to engage and sustain the elements that have come together to make you feel this way. For example, if you have started an exercise regimen, lost an amount of unneeded weight, and now feel great, keep on exercising. If you have started a passionate and thrilling relationship with a significant other person, keep on seeing this person. Whatever this wonderful energy booster may be, it can be analyzed and maintained. The passion and energy of a new romance, for example, does not need to fade to zero if you keep kindling the fire of your and your partner's intimacy and love.

This will be the kind of fire that is also capable of taking you up to another level of awareness in your life. This will not be the slow-burning, house-warming fire made for the long night; this will be a big, blazing bonfire made for celebration and elation in the moment. So, let it blaze. As mentioned, it will not, and cannot, continue to blaze in its magnificent glory throughout the night. You will let your fire burn lower at some point. But not right now. This fire that you will be feeling has wonderful transformative power that will push you where you need to be. Let it burn! Even if you fail, the golden memories will be worth it. Live, love, laugh! You will be unstoppable. Make the most of your fire, passion, desire, and time.

Prince of Wands

Strength - Persistence - Progress - Control
Poise - Dignity - Grandeur - Resolve

"It's not how much you have that makes people
look up to you. It's who you are."
- Elvis Presley

When you draw the Prince of Wands, you will soon be
starting or continuing a journey or quest with power,
purpose, and ample energy. You will be advancing slowly
and steadily, and you will be well equipped for long-term
forward progress. It will be early in your particular pursuit,
and you should take time to feel the divine purpose flowing
around you. You will be pulled forward and guided by the
Universe's power and protection. As such, this card is
encouraging you to continue in your life to go steadily
forward with whatever it is you are doing because you are
doing it right.

Be careful not to let this energy turn into vanity and
arrogance. Do not be overconfident in yourself or overly
ambitious. While it is wonderful to have a strong, positive
sense and image of yourself, there is a line which you can
dangerously cross that will lead you into conceit as well as
all the related problems that follow from taking your energy
into this place. As you do this, you will find the beautiful
and productive balance that on one hand recognizes,
celebrates, and uses your strength and beauty, but on the
other hand, realizes that all these things are great gifts of the

Universe. Your fire will blaze with greater intensity and much greater heights than ever is possible when you indulge in conceit, pride, and vanity.

Your journey onward will be wonderful. Let the mighty lion visualized in this card pull you toward greatness rather than whipping your own horses toward selfish goals. Stay the course; let go of the reins. Do not let your pride and ambition make you think that you can control the lion because it is impossible and trying to do so will hurt you dearly. Greatness is ahead! Bring it on! Open your strong arms to accept it. You can handle it. Persistence and conquest. Look out world, here you come!

Queen of Wands

Rest - Reflection - Satisfaction - Achievement
Grace - Beauty - Intuition - Pleasure

"Follow your passions, follow your heart,
and the things that you need will come."
- Elizabeth Taylor

When you draw the Queen of Wands, the energy and fire that you have been putting into something will soon be ending. This will be a good and glorious conclusion that will leave you and your vitality in a wonderful place. You will feel confident and empowered to keep going forward in your life. As you do this, this card also reminds you to trust your intuition. What you feel, rather than what you see, will be what counts. Be prepared to indulge your royal, mystical, and graceful life force. You will be bound for even more wonderful things!

Even now when you are not quite at the conclusion of your current quest, it will be good for you to close your eyes, sit still, and contemplate your achievement as pictured on this card. Your efforts will have made you stronger. Once your conclusion has taken place, take time to draw your energy inward and breathe. You will be satisfied, rested, and ready for new challenges that are sure to come your way. You should not revert to stress and strain or in any other negative energy as you cultivate grace and royal power. Nevertheless, you will need to be careful with your energy, for you have the ability to destroy others with just a look. Also, you will need to check yourself of any pointless jealousy that may arise in you. This card is reaffirming that you and your life are both unique and wonderful. You will be wasting your energy if you engage in any type of comparison or contrast with others.

You should be using your powers of clairvoyance and intuition and connecting your vitality with the unseen vibrations of the Universe. Be at peace with yourself and your life. Shut out the chaos that may be around you as you nurture the royalty and calmness of the great cats (also pictured on this card.) These top predators are not neurotic like we humans. They are noble. They do not spend their energy worrying about dangers like mice do. Neither should you. Be noble, not neurotic. All hail the Queen!

Knight of Wands

Energy - Belief - Strength - Power
Nobility - Idealism - Progress - Conquest

"The meaning of life is not simply to exist, to survive;
it is to move ahead, to go up, to achieve, to conquer."
- Arnold Schwarzenegger

When you draw the Knight of Wands, you will soon be charging forward with ample energy and boldness toward your goals and aspirations. You will feel strong, stronger than you may have ever felt before. You will be able to take on your enemies, be victorious, and continue valiantly onward. You will not let any negative energy that may have held you down in your recent or distant past enter your life. You will look inside yourself and find the fierce energy of battle, protection, and conquest. These energies will be needed for some significant purpose in your life, and this card is reminding you of this as well as encouraging your forward progress.

You will be unstoppable. Your fire will be burning brightly, and you will be full of energy and vitality. It will be a time for you to be bold, take risks, and be active. Importantly, it will be a time to stand up for what is right and true. You should not waste this energy on trivial or harmful things. Keep truth, justice, honour as your highest goals. Act with the courage and resolve that are part of the Knight's code. Be careful that you do not lower yourself for anyone's pleasure or self-serving ambitions. Many people who are not as noble as you will want to bring you down because they are jealous of you. Brush them aside and fill your life with fellow knights who see each other as equals upholding similar values, missions, and goals.

You should be using your energy to make the Universe a better place not only because you are a part of the wonders but also because you are a strong, active part of it all. You are needed and wanted. You are a noble and key part of the divine energy ever flowing between destruction and creation. You must protect the good kingdom. Charge forward! Cut down those forces that oppose you and your noble knight's mission. Look behind you and quiet any past calamities or personal qualms that may be threatening or hindering your present quest. Then turn around and push forward. Battle on!

Cups

"If I comprehend all mysteries and all knowledge
and have faith to move mountains,
but do not have love, I am nothing."
- Saint Paul

After you have drawn your card from the Wands, the next card to draw is from the Cups. Shuffle the Cups according to your preference. Remember also to clear the deck from past energy by some means such as knocking on the deck as described on page 15. Once drawn, this card will then be placed in the top left side of the pentacle layout, below and to the left of your Trump card.

The suit of Cups represents the element water. You are physically mostly made of water, and our planet is mostly covered by water, not land. Water is the great, life-giving blessing to both our planet and yourself. Consider that you can survive for a long time without food but not without water. The same goes for your emotions and emotional life. If you try to live life without emotional involvement, you will have no life at all, and you *will* wither and die the same as a houseplant that is not watered.

Your emotions give personal meaning to all things. You do not see the world the way the world is; you see the world the way you are. And the way you are is a product of your emotional involvement in your life. This is easy to see in how you respond to a rainy day, for example. If you are depressed, the rain will seem bleak and dreary. If you are in love, the rain will seem romantic, life-giving, and wonderful.

Water can and needs to change forms. It must cycle through liquid, vapour, and ice to keep it fresh and flowing. Likewise, your emotions need to change from one state to another as you live your life. Just as happiness and elation cannot last forever, the same is true with sadness and despair. Like water, your emotional state needs its cycle of renewal and flow; otherwise, personal problems are bound to occur just like in the stagnation of water.

As the moon pulls the oceans to make tides, Universal forces outside of you push and pull your emotional life. Think of this and consider that your emotional ups and downs are both natural and necessary.

As you shuffle the Cups meditate on the element water and how essential and fundamental it is to you. Picture in your mind's eye some remembrance of water that you have experienced such as a river, lake, or ocean. Do not work too hard at this; let the imagery come to you. Breathe deeply thanking the Universe for water and asking for advice for your emotional wellness from the Tarot.

Divine essence of water, please help me at this time in my life to know what is best for my heart and my emotional life. Dear and wonderful Universe, what does my heart need to hear and understand right now to best help my own life and the lives of others?

Ace of Cups

Confidence - Attraction - Strength - Reassurance
Purpose - Beauty - Enjoyment - Inspiration

"Love yourself first, then everything else falls in line."
- Lucille Ball

When you draw the Ace of Cups, you will soon be feeling the self-love and confidence that come from reaffirming that you are special, loved, and filled with divine purpose. This confident, productive, and positive emotional state will carry you forward in whatever lies ahead for you. You should be going forward with an image of how wonderful and beautiful you are. Further, you should be eliminating or silencing any person in your life who dares to bring you down with horrible, insulting words and names. Finally, as part of this confidence and self-love, you should not be saying bad things about yourself, even in a joking manner.

Your life and love will flourish as you refrain from putting yourself down and refrain from associating with anyone who puts you down. It is good to love yourself. It is never good to dwell in self-loathing. While this card reminds you to practice saying positive things about yourself, this card also is also asking you to consider what is the main thing in your life that brings you joy, pride, and positive purpose? Your emotional wellness will depend on getting more of whatever this. Perhaps it is something as simple as spending more time walking your dog or playing with your children. Perhaps it is music, dance, or art. Maybe it is exercise or meditation. If you have been neglecting activities and pursuits that enrich your emotional life in positive ways, get back into doing these things. This card is reassuring you that you have many fantastic blessings in your emotional life forthcoming, but it is also saying that all these good things must start with you.

You will be stepping forward in your life with a strong, brave, and big heart, and you will not need to worry about someone supporting you. You will support, nurture, and love *yourself*. No one can do this for you, and when you do this, your life will blossom. Other people who contribute to your emotional wellness such as friends, family, and lovers will come along for the ride. They will *want* to be with you and will contribute to your emotional wellness as long as you are not expecting them to do the work that you should be doing yourself. Smile, laugh, sing! You will be satisfied, strong, bold, and beautiful. You *are* awesome, lovely, and wonderful!

Two of Cups

Love - Happiness - Intimacy - Affection
Bonding - Fulfilment - Beauty - Kindness

"The greatest thing that you will ever learn
is to love and be loved in return."
- Natalie Cole

When you draw the Two of Cups, you are about to enter a time in your life that will bring lasting goodness, enrichment, and love. This may be meeting someone who will become a long-term blessing to you and your life. You may find a position or job that will bring you great joy and happiness. Regardless of what happens, you will soon be with another person, place, thing, or idea, and this relationship will bring you harmony, contentment, and love. Welcome this with open arms, a hopeful heart, and clear mind. There is nothing better than this feeling, and it is possible to live in love. This is to say that you can be "in love" for all the days of your life.

This card is telling you to be receptive to this type of intimate emotional attachment. As you do this and realize that love is as real as your feelings, all potential cynicism about love will vanish. You need love-based bonding with people, places, things, and ideas in your life. Otherwise, your life will become boring, stale, and brittle with little emotional meaning. It may be that you only need to be reminded how blessed you are to be with someone or something that has been, and can continue to be, the love of your life. In other words if this is the case, the "something new" will be falling in love again with someone or something from which you have become detached.

Whatever happens for you, it will be wonderful to let your life fill up with the happiness and joy that love brings. Also, as you take time to understand how powerful these feelings are and how capable they are of transforming you, this wonderful state will continue to make your life blossom like a flowering plant. And as a flowering plant needs to be nurtured, so too will you need to nurture your love to ensure that it keeps on flowering rather than withering and dying. Keep in mind that although the Universe will be playing an important role, you will need to do your part as well in reaching out and making all this happen as it should and can be. Love is, in the end, all you really need.

Three of Cups

Friendship - Celebration - Happiness - Support
Encouragement - Laughter - Cheer - Togetherness

"It's so nice to meet an old friend and pass the time away;
talk about the hometown, a million miles away."
- Gordon Lightfoot

When you draw the Three of Cups, you are about to be in a wonderful emotional state. This will be a time to celebrate and enjoy your close circle of friends and family or reconnect with life-long friends whom you have not seen for many years. There may not be a big gathering and celebration such as a wedding or anniversary. More likely this will be a time for smaller and closely-knit bonds to be reaffirmed and enjoyed. You may also be meeting new people in your near future with whom you will become close, so be open to this possibility as always, but even more so as you go forward from here.

As mentioned, this happy emotional state will be the product of getting together with close friends or family members for lunch or something similar. You will be happy, and you will share this happiness as only is possible with these important others who are in your life. Life is meant to be enjoyed and not just endured. There are and will be plenty of conflicts and troubles in your life. But there are also plenty of rest stops, dinners to enjoy, and beverages to joyfully and socially drink. Your life will be richer, more engaging, and more complete when you make time to experience these things. This card is reminding you to not make excuses; it will be time for you to help the Universe make it happen. It can be as simple as sending an invitation by phone or text.

If you have developed some habits like eating at your desk while you work through the lunch hour, change these isolation-inducing lifestyle/workplace practices and routines. Something as simple as a coffee break is needed and wanted. The thing is to stop working and stressing for a while and enjoy a break. There will be time for the work to get done, and ironically you will be far more productive, getting more done because of the added energy and creativity that others can and will bring you. Perhaps no true break and celebration can be had when you are alone. The social aspect of a break and celebration needs to be there. So go ahead and do some of this. Be sociable! Laugh, hug, smile, talk, enjoy! Cheers!

Four of Cups

Completion - Celebration - Pride - Happiness
Satisfaction — Achievement - Affirmation - Joy

"What is happiness? It is the feeling that power
is growing and resistance is overcome."
- Friedrich Nietzsche

When you draw the Four of Cups, your life will soon be in a very good emotional place. This will happen because you will have a sense of completion, satisfaction, and perhaps closure on some aspect of your life. You will be feeling that all is well. You will be able to sit back for a while and enjoy your workmanship, as when you complete a renovation project on your home. You know that there are things that you would have done differently now that it is complete, but this should not stop you from celebrating your achievement, feeling good, and being proud of yourself. Whatever it may be, you will reach a new level of personal contentment that you have largely brought about through your own noble and well-guided efforts.

The feeling of personal achievement is like no other. It is a great motivating force positively affecting your emotional life and general wellness. This goodness is multiplied when your achievement brings you closer to your highest aims in life. So enjoy these times and let them build resilience and confidence in you. Some things in the Universe that bring you happiness seemingly fall into your lap, but that is something on which you should not count. If you keep applying yourself, you will have a far more reliable way to bring this kind of happiness into your life, and you will be better able to journey onward with confidence, success, and emotional wellness.

The joyful times such as these that will be coming into your life can lift you up to higher levels of awareness and happiness. Nevertheless, be prepared to reach one of those plateaus on which you will travel for a time before another hill or valley intervenes with your path. It will be best for you to travel on this new plateau of happiness and awareness for a time, letting your life fill with the goodness and contentment of reaching this plateau! You should walk freely and easily; you deserve this. Do not spoil it by worrying about all the things that are still to be done or how you would do them differently if you had a second chance. Feel good. Feel positive. Enjoy the moment and all of what you have accomplished. Great job! Awesome work!

Five of Cups

Despondency - Emptiness - Loss - Depression
Sadness - Grief - Melancholy - Discontent

"Sunrise doesn't last all morning. A cloudburst doesn't last
all day. It's not always going to be grey.
All things pass, all things must pass away."
- George Harrison

When you draw the Five of Cups, you will soon be
feeling intense loss, emptiness, and sadness. Something in
your life will be going away or ending. This something may
be a job loss, the end of a relationship, or a close friend
moving away from your neigbourhood. Whatever it may be,
you will go through a time of feeling empty, sad, and
desolated. It will seem as if all your cups of happiness have
been drained. You will need to keep in mind that life is like
this sometimes. It is not your fault, and you are not being
punished. You will have to deal with your emotions, so do
not repress your feelings. Cry. Do *not* deny your anger,
grief, or sadness. You must go through the various phases of
the grieving process.

As you go through this time in your life, do not get stuck
in any part of your sadness and sorrow; keep moving
through. Trust that this will be a temporary situation for
you. It will not be destructive or final unless you make it so.
Consider that you are still in possession of your cups even
though they are not now full and overflowing, as seen in this
card's imagery. Your empty cups will again fill to

overflowing in time. Do not throw them away. For example, do not promise yourself that you will never fall in love again. Remember a basic truism: you cannot know what happiness is unless you also know what unhappiness is. Aim to arm yourself with whatever it may be that will help you through this time such as applying the healing power of water. There is a reason for the watery background of this card. You will benefit from a long, hot shower or bath. You will heal as you stand by the ocean and hear the surf or walk along the shores of a river or stream. Solace, support, and comfort will come to you. All things will pass if you let them.

Unfortunately, there must be times like this. It is part of the cost of being alive and engaged in life. Life is never simple and not meant to be easy. Although you may feel responsible for bringing yourself to this position, do not continue to blame yourself. As you let the sun go down on your sorrow, a new sun will rise on a better tomorrow. As you embrace hope, engage in prayer or meditation, your emotional state will turn around before too long. You heart will heal and fill with happiness again!

Six of Cups

Love - Happiness - Joy - Comfort
Delight- Gladness - Celebration - Merriment

"Let your love shine!"
- Larry E. Williams

When you draw the Six of Cups, you will soon be in a very good emotional place. You will feel intense joy and happiness for no particular reason at all. Everything will seem to come together for you! Do not worry about why this is happening and enjoy the moment. Do not sabotage yourself and your happiness by making up excuses why you cannot be happy and joyful. There are likely a number of reasons for this state of affairs in your life, but not everything needs to be figured out or analyzed. This card confirms that there *is* magic in the air. Let it come to you!

You need times like this in your life, and times like these often come to you when other elements in your life can be worrisome or problematic. The key is to not let any of these worries stop you from enjoying the happiness and joy that will be forthcoming in your life. Let your love flow and shine! Count your blessings, not your troubles. Realize that most of your troubles are self-generated, and your emotional worries are not as you are making them to be. Regardless of your current circumstances, you will soon be experiencing wonderful, uplifting elation and happiness that will be nearly impossible to put into words.

This card is reminding you to be receptive to joy and celebration whether it is with familiar people or with new people you may be meeting soon. Who knows where this may lead? It will not lead *anywhere* if you do not engage in and remain open to the wondrous possibilities. Therefore, do not let anything intervene, especially excuses or any practiced negativity that may have been plaguing your emotional life. Why not look up the song "Let Your Love Flow" by the Bellamy Brothers that is present in the opening quotation for this card? But, do not listen to it. Sing along at the top of your voice! Be joyful! Let your love shine!

Seven of Cups

Overindulgence - Addiction - Loss - Waste
Excess – Gluttony - Obsession - Preoccupation

"Everything in moderation: including moderation."
- Oscar Wilde

When you draw the Seven of Cups, you will soon need to be very careful with your emotional state. Further, you will need to make changes to your behaviour or lifestyle. For whatever reason, you will have strayed off course and will need corrective action. The corrective action will be moderation. Perhaps you have been relying too much on the aid of external substances such as drugs, alcohol, and food *to make* you feel happy? There is nothing wrong with any of these things in themselves, but these things, like nearly everything out there that can enhance the pleasure of your life, are open to abuse. With abuse, these things change from their true function into something that degrades your emotional life rather than enhancing it.

As you examine your life to see what needs to be moderated in order to rebalance your happiness and emotional wellness, you will be well on your way to engaging the corrective action needed. It could be an excess of watching sports on television or other types of shows such as soap operas or cable news. It could be an excess of exercise or suntanning. It may be an excess of alcohol, drugs, or junk food. Maybe you are being too ambitious or overly obsessed with another's affection. Whatever it is, as you moderate these pleasure-seeking diversions, happiness and wellness will return to you.

   This card is *not* telling you that you need a complete makeover or change of direction in your life. The Seven of Cups is more about encouraging you to make those smaller, but important, lifestyle changes that will bring moderation and control into your life. As you do this, be careful not to switch one overindulgence with another one. Do not simply switch from excess coffee to excess tea, for example. Also, do not eliminate the things in your life that bring you joy; instead, start enjoying yourself and your life more through the practical magic that is moderation. You have enough self-control to do this. Changes must be made, and all will be well. Aim for balance, wellness, and happiness.
Start today!

Eight of Cups

Self-pity - Depression - Bleakness - Dreariness
Cheerlessness - Sullenness - Displeasure - Sadness

"I have made peace with the things that I thought
were weaknesses or flaws. I like them. Your imperfections
are what make you beautiful."
- Sandra Bullock

When you draw the Eight of Cups, your emotional life
will soon be in a state of transition and general emptiness.
You will feel that something is missing because something
will be missing. Perhaps you have been indulging in
self-pity? Self-pity is never good for you or your life.
Self-pity stifles all joy and stops your life from moving
forward. Helen Keller, the famous woman who overcame
her deafness and blindness to live a full and active life, calls
self-pity the worst of all emotions. Whatever it is that is
missing from your life should be relatively easy to identify
and remedy. If you follow this card's advice, your
emotional wellness will come back to you with more
happiness, goodness, and fulfilment.

Your first step toward wellness will be to look inward
and take responsibility for your emotional life. As you stop
blaming others or the Universe for your condition, and as
you stop saying things such as, "I always have bad luck"
and "I am cursed," you will be on your way to *making* your
life and your emotional state more satisfying and happier.
As you change your self-talk to build a stronger and truer

sense of yourself, and as you stop contrasting yourself with others, you will start to build or rebuild that special, unique, and loving relationship with the Universe that is so crucial to all aspects of your emotional wellness.

This card is here to remind you that this relationship between you and your life needs to nurtured by *you*; you are responsible for yourself and your happiness—no one else is. And fundamentally, this is what you want. You do *not* want your happiness and wellness to be dependent on anyone else. Although life can seem very unfair most days, this unfairness is only an illusion. So look closely at what may be causing this vacant feeling in your life and aim to correct it so that those empty cups as pictured on this card can be filled to overflowing once again. You will need a change of perspective. Choose to be glad. Make cheerfulness and gratitude a habit! As the novelist George Eliot pointed out, "Wear a smile and have friends; wear a frown and have wrinkles." Smile! Be yourself! Be happy.

Nine of Cups

Positivity - Goodness - Relief - Rest
Contentment - Celebration - Compliments - Bliss

"I try for excellence, not perfection.
Perfection belongs to God."
- Michael J Fox

When you draw the Nine of Cups, your emotional life will soon be in great shape with many good things coming your way. You will feel like you are getting rewarded for your steady and true progress. You likely have had many struggles, conflicts, and ordeals to get this point, and you should take note that you would not appreciate times like this unless you *have had* your share of battles and confrontations. Although you will not be resting or relaxing yet, you will start to feel the relief that comes when you have turned a corner on some tougher times.

Perhaps you will be finally getting over a divorce or some other heartbreak. Perhaps you will be starting to love yourself again after a period of self-loathing. Whatever it may be, keep going forward from the past and keep doing the things that are bringing you fulfilment and joy. Reaffirm yourself and your life's purpose and worth. This card reminds you that are a child of the Universe, and the Universe wants you to feel good about yourself. In addition, it reaffirms that you need to love yourself before you can love anyone else. Your life is full of ups and downs, hills and valleys, and all of these times have purpose and meaning. It will be a good time for you to learn from your journey and try your best to avoid the hazards that befell your previous footsteps.

This card also is cautioning you about those perfectionistic thoughts that can constantly bring you down. You will spoil so much by never being happy even if your cups are as full and neatly arranged as is illustrated on this card. Do *not* say, "Damn, everything is great; I have nine full cups, how do I get a perfect 10?" Be grateful and enjoy the wonderful place that you will be in. Understand that it will not last forever, but do not worry about that. Sit back and look with pride and joy at yourself and your life. Yes, there will be more work to do, but do not let that spoil your moment. Be grateful that you are on the right path and keep on loving yourself. You are awesome!

Ten of Cups

Happiness - Exultation - Gloriousness - Significance
Fullness - Wellness - Appreciation - Pleasure

"Gratitude is wine for the soul. Go on. Get drunk!"
- Rumi

When you draw the Ten of Cups, your emotional life will soon be in a very, very good place. Your heart will be full and overflowing with positive vibrations that come at a major milestone point in your life such as getting married to the right person, seeing your children graduate from school, paying off a car loan, or retiring with style, fulfilment, and health. You should be grateful for whatever it is that has brought you to this place, and you should make the most of this time by not letting any fears or worries about the future or present bring you down. These peak moments need to be treasured and stored inside you. These good memories will help you carry on when your life seems to be going nowhere or downhill.

Feel and enjoy the wonderful sense of completion, wholeness, and goodness that is coming to your life. You may sense that this is as good as it gets. Indeed, this *may* be one of those times where your emotional life *is* as good as it gets! There are limits to how high and how long you can fly. Your life will have plenty of emotional problems and pains as you go forward. But for now, do not waste these high points that you have achieved; drink them in, breathe deeply and say, "Thank you Universe!" If you are not yet in the habit of living with gratitude, start now when it will be so easy. This will also show you how gratitude works to sustain your bliss and emotional wellness for longer stretches of time than are otherwise possible.

You will see that more thankful you are, the more emotional wealth you gain, and the more often these times of wholesome happiness will come to you. Unfortunately, gratitude is always under attack by those forces that try to keep you down, scared, and nervous about the future. This is especially true when living in our capitalist and materialist world. You can be happy with a lot less if you do not constantly worry and fret about having more possessions, being more secure, and contrasting yourself to others. So as you travel forward, celebrate and enjoy! Sleep contented with no bad dreams!

Princess of Cups

Contentment - Pleasure - Love - Happiness
Wonder - Friendship/Family - Abundance - Sharing

"Spread love where ever you go;
let no one ever come to you without leaving happier."
- Mother Teresa

When you draw the Princess of Cups, you will soon be in a wonderful emotional state; you will also be sharing your happiness and joy with others in your life. Let your contentment and loving presence shine! Beware that there are others who will be jealous of your happiness, beauty, and blessings. You will see this jealousy in the people who will try to put you down in one way or another. But do not let these people get you down. Only you know the true cost of becoming who you are and all the hardships and difficulties that you have gotten through to get to this wonderful, beautiful place.

You may be called upon to help or assist someone who is going through emotional difficulties. You should have no problems doing this. Furthermore, doing so will bless your own life with more joy, contentment, and happiness. A danger for you is to become vain or excessively prideful. As such, you may become too particular with whom you share your gifts and your happiness. Be aware of this, and how it can be avoided by trusting your intuition. Also, recall how this danger can be avoided by staying aloof, regal, and simply avoiding those bottom feeders who would like to pull you down into their muck and sludge.

This card is telling you to stay reserved, but keep busy with your princess-like role of being beautiful, kind, loving, and giving to those around you. You have traveled many difficult paths to get to this place, but others do not see this. Your kindness has been tested again and again. Nevertheless, as you keep on this path with strength and resolve, staying kind and loving, you will continue to help those around you who may or may not appreciate all that you are doing and all that you have done. Stay true to yourself and your life, and you will stay happy and joyful with all the gifts that you have been given and have worked hard, against many odds, to maintain. You *are* a great blessing to the Universe!

Prince of Cups

Strength - Happiness - Engagement - Positivity
Joy - Excitement - Resolve - Composure

"I believe that we are here for each other,
not against each other. Everything comes from an
understanding that you are gift in my life."
- John Denver

When you draw the Prince of Cups, you will soon be
feeling both confident and sturdy in all parts of your
emotional life. You will feel bold and will want to engage
and revel in your strong feelings. As you let this emotional
happiness carry you to a new level, you will feel ready to
fly! You can trust that all will be well, and you should feel
good about yourself. Nevertheless, beware of the danger of
becoming too proud and disdainful. Also, do not become
like the ungrateful prince who takes all of his goodness and
environmental blessings for granted. When you stay humble
and grateful for all your wonderful gifts and your
prince-like strength and position, you will be able to seize
more wondrous possibilities in your future.

This card is telling you to take time to reflect on your
life. Go for a brisk walk or bike ride. Feel your strong
energy. Consider that you have immense reserves of
youthful strength and strong emotion: a true crown prince!
But also consider that these parts of yourself need to be
directed toward the benefit of others; your strength and
valour can become dangerous if misdirected. Like the bold

prince pictured in this card, you have a lot of influence on the emotional lives of others, so be careful and use your influence wisely for both yourself and others.

In spite of all the good things coming to your emotional wellness, you will still be needing your strength, determination, and toughness. You will have to do what must be done and some of this will be difficult. For example, you may have to put down a beloved pet due to its advanced age, or you may need to discipline a wayward child. Whatever it may be, you will need to be resilient, brave, and firm. Remember that it will be essential for you to not only act with strength and positive force but also essential for you to feel the consequences of your actions as a human being. It will be okay to cry. In cases such as these, crying is not a sign of weakness; it is a sign of deep strength and emotional wellness. Fly high! Bring it on! You got this!

Queen of Cups

Grace - Happiness - Wellness - Compassion
Influence - Goodness - Benevolence - Balance

"I do things differently; I don't go by
a rule book; I lead from the heart."
- Princess Diana

When you draw the Queen of Cups, your emotional life will soon be glorious. You will have grace, power, and strength, and you will be in a position to bestow your gifts on others. You should not hesitate to share your emotional wellness with others but be queenly in *how* you share your gifts. Do not lower yourself to commonness. A queen engages with others much lower than herself, but when she does so, she does not debase herself, ever. The Queen of Cups also does not engage in neurotic and petty worries and neither should you.

As you radiate love and emotional power from this high place and exercise your queenly qualities such as compassion, kindness, grace, and nurturing, you will enrich both you own emotional life and the emotional lives of others. This is not to say that you will not have to work hard at avoiding unnecessary anger, personal vendettas, unforgiving violent thoughts, and all manners of pointless aggression. In fact, you may have to work harder at this in the near future as you travel forward. A queen's life is not an easy life! Nevertheless, all will be well if you keep aiming for serenity, poise, dignity, generosity, understanding, and kindness from your queenly throne.

In short, this card is encouraging you to not only be soft and caring but also regal and somewhat aloof. From this position, you will radiate good vibrations that will carry forward and will keep things orderly and noble rather than chaotic and neurotic. As mentioned previously, do not hesitate to involve yourself in noble causes, especially in helping others and letting your influence of goodness and power radiate outward in your life and into the Universe. Keep in mind, however, that you cannot fix every problem. Give yourself queenly distance from those unsolvable problems. All hail the kind, loving, and beautiful Queen!

Knight of Cups

Bliss - Accomplishment - Victory - Strength
Celebration - Honour - Purity - Wonder

"The longer I go about living, I see it's
the relationships that are the most meaningful."
- William Shatner

When you draw the Knight of Cups, you will be entering
a time in your life when your emotional state will be
wonderful, advantageous, and fulfilling. You will feel like
you are capable of flying high into the air because you will
be so astonishingly full of positive emotion. This emotional
high will be associated with something wonderful such as
falling in love with the right person, gaining a promotion for
which you have been working, or some other delightful
event.

You will not need to occupy yourself with unnecessary
worry or too much caution. You will be well poised to go
forward and have things work out for you bringing more
positive emotion to you. This will be because you have been
pursuing something for a while and have gone through
many tests and ordeals to get to this place. As such, you
have earned this happiness, wellness, and reward. But even
at this time, be careful to not become conceited or too
pleased with yourself and the role that you have played.
Remember that you can only take 50% of the credit for all
of your successes. The other 50% belongs to luck.
Nevertheless, this card is all about *your* success and

happiness. Let your life fill with this wonderful, powerful mixture!

Soon the Knight in you will get uninterested with life in this royal court, and you will crave more adventures. These high points of bliss and victory cannot be sustained for long periods of time. Nevertheless, this card is telling you to make sure that you enjoy the parade, the glory, the wonderment of the good times and the good places that you will be entering. You will spread your beauty and love. Others will look up to you as a shining example of humanity! As is pictured on this card, do not remove all of the armour that you have on, but lighten it up and let those safe, warm breezes of home caress your skin. Fairy tales can and do come true.

Swords

"You have power over your mind—not outside events.
Realize this, and you will find strength."
- Marcus Aurelius

After you draw from the Cups, the next suit from which to draw a card is the Swords. The Swords align with the element of air. The Swords are about your mind and your thoughts as opposed to your heart and your feelings. There is a balance to be struck between your mind and your heart as you journey through life. There are times when you should listen to your head and times when you need to listen to your heart. Neither side is better than the other. Ideally, they are complementary and well balanced.

Imbalance between your head and heart creates consequences that are not good for you. For example, if you rarely listen to your heart, you can become cold, unfeeling, and dangerous to yourself and others around you. On the other hand, if you rarely listen to your head, you can become chaotic, depressed, and also a danger to yourself and others around you.

Another thing to consider with your human mind is that there are at least three discernable aspects to your mind's amazing construction: your conscious, your subconscious, and your conscience. The three elements work in conjunction with each other and are all important to your life. If these elements of your mind are out of balance with each other, problems will result.

In the Tarot, the suit of Swords clearly makes the connection with the most iconic of all weapons: the sword. This is appropriate because your mind *is* your greatest weapon. You are not like other animals that have claws and teeth. Your mind has been and will continue to be the powerful weapon that you need to take on all of your adversaries. Your mind is far more important than any brute strength in tackling enemies and forces that oppose you. Thus, a sword is an apt representation for your mind.

When shuffling and drawing a card from the Swords, think about the element air and how it surrounds you and nurtures you. Breathe in deeply and slowly exhale thanking the Universe for this wonderful element. Let your thoughts be still, in a relaxed and open-minded state. Do not concentrate as if you are doing a math problem. Rather let the Universe gently into your head asking for advice and blessing.

Divine spirit of air, what do I need think about at this time in my journey and quest? Is my mind missing something? What decisions do I need to make that will be as cutting and powerful as a sword? Dear Universe, help me to think clearly and effectively at this time.

Ace of Swords

Success - Engagement - Confidence - Power
Victory - Focus - Conviction - Clout

"My life is a testament to believing that if you want
something you can make it. I wasn't going to be a stupid
girl singer. I wanted to be more than that."
- Stevie Nicks

When you draw the Ace of Swords, your mind will soon
be focused and rigid in its determination, confidence, and
aim. This will not be a time for compromise. It will be a
time to strike forward with your energy and enthusiasm.
You will be on the right path, so do not swerve away from
it. Be confident and aware of your abilities, strengths, and
weaknesses. But focus more on your strengths rather than
your weaknesses. The obstacles in your path are not going
to stop you, yet it is still good to consider and recognize
them because this will help you as you journey forward.

You and your mind have come to this place with a lot of
power and potential. Trust that you will carry forward in the
conflicts that you will be facing. Imagine that the Universe
is handing you the great sword of power to assist you. Focus
on just one goal at this time and make it a grand goal.
Consider what is the one thing that you would most like for
your life. Do not make this about your emotional life,
however. Focus on your mind and what your mind is good
at doing and has been doing well. For example, if you are a
good organizer and planner, you should engage in some

career or activity that uses your mental acuity for these activities.

There is perhaps no greater weapon than confidence, and this card is giving you more confidence. So do not let doubts in. Hold your head up keeping your thoughts and energies on successful outcomes. There are bound to be obstacles out there, but you need to stay focused and positive: no doubts, no despair, and no depression are allowed! Trust that you will get through and be victorious. Grab that big sword and charge forward. Your enemies and adversaries will run as you give that mighty battle roar that says, "I am here! I am unstoppable! I am strong! I will not fail!" Take up this sword of unyielding confidence. Nurture and treasure it. Let it take you forward. Stay the course. Forward march! Charge!

Two of Swords

Stalemate - Deadlock - Standstill - Stubbornness
Inflexibility - Obstinacy - Standoff - Impasse

"Compromise is the best and cheapest lawyer."
- North American Proverb

When you draw the Two of Swords, your mind will soon be facing a conflict where a singular opposing force will be challenging you and your way forward in life. This will be either a personal dilemma between two choices/goals or an interpersonal conflict with another person. This will be a conflict where a compromise should be made to end the struggle. It may also be a long-standing stalemate that has been causing you more grief than joy. Look both inward and outward as you consider this blockage and stalemate; be ready to compromise.

As mentioned, this card is encouraging you to seek a compromise with whatever it is that you are battling. Consider this battle as tie where no side wins, and life carries on. The goodness of your situation can be seen in the bright blossom at the center of the crossed swords as pictured on this card. So, although there are times when you need to be stubborn and firm, this will be a time for your mind to be both open and receptive to all possible means of resolution. You may be at odds with a family member or co-worker. If so, you need to be willing to consider the other's point of view as well as be willing to negotiate. With conciliation you will be able to reach a satisfactory conclusion. You may have two conflicting personal goals that are not attainable at the same time; if so, you will need to find a way to balance them by altering each one slightly, rather than giving up either goal entirely.

Harmony and balance will be coming back into your life and mind. So focus on that. While fights and opposition are necessary to build strength and stamina, a strong and wise person knows when call a truce and make peace. Nevertheless, keep in mind that this card is *not* calling for surrender. This card is about compromise and peace. Find the middle way. Life is full of all kinds of battles and the worst ones are the ones that go on and on, like an intergenerational feud. Often all that is needed is a step back from the conflict. You will make peace with yourself and make peace with your adversary. Peace is good. Peace will allow you to move forward.

Three of Swords

Sorrow - Hopelessness - Depression - Distress
Loss - Suffering - Collapse - Ruin

"Although the world is full of suffering,
it is also full of overcoming it."
- Helen Keller

When you draw the Three of Swords, your mind will soon be overwhelmed with sadness and sorrow. This distress will be difficult for you and your mind. You will be thinking that you cannot hold yourself together and that all is lost. You may even be wishing you had not been born. Although you will be feeling isolated and helpless, this is not the case. You are never forsaken or not wanted: accept and act upon this. You are mentally stronger than you think you are. Your mind will only break if you lose faith and hope.

You will endure a portion of sorrow and mental anguish in your life. Loss and grief are a natural part of life, and you must get through the grieving process each time you experience personal loss. As you rediscover that there is a purpose to your life and trust the grand design of the Universe, you will overcome the difficult times that are upcoming in your life. How can it be that all that wonder and life that is encapsulated in your own creation be worthless? As you stop feeling sorry for yourself and regain your self-worth, you will find a way out of your tragic situation.

This card from the Swords is telling you that you will have to use your head and logic to reason with yourself. Shakespeare called logic and reason, "adversity's sweet milk." This is to say, the logical side your mind is built for overcoming the emotional sadness that can envelope and destroy not only your mind but also your life itself. This will be one of those times when you will need to use this logical, rational, and essential aspect of your mind. It is okay to ask the Universe for better times; especially, it is okay to ask for strength to overcome your sadness. But you will need to be an active part of this process as well. So, you will need to get out there and do something positive. This sadness will not last forever unless you stop going forward and lose all hope by falling into the metaphoric pit of despair. Take one step at time. You and your mind will get through this. This sadness of yours has a purpose, but it is *not* the purpose of your life.

Four of Swords

Wellness - Insight - Strength - Teamwork
Reward - Advancement - Friendliness - Prize

"If it's bitter at the start, then it's sweeter at the end."
- Madonna

When you draw the Four of Swords, your mind will be peaceful, accurate, and powerful. You will discover solutions to your problem and conflicts. This process will both strengthen and advance your mind and intellect. In addition, it will bring peace, friendship, and rewards to your life. There will also be a strong element of teamwork and cooperation with your success and wellness. You and your team are headed for bonuses and progress! Your ability to focus on the solution as well as being able to target your efforts on what needs to be done will be highly discernable and effective. Carry forward with a motivated and determined mind, an eager work ethic, and the keenness of your intellect.

This will also be a time for rest and reflection; this will be coming to you after a period of mental stress and persistent or serious troubles. You will soon be able to reflect on the truth of this old truism: "No struggle; no strength." Struggle is big part of the human condition and a necessary aspect of your freedom. Your struggles reaffirm that you are in charge of your life and destiny. So do not wish for the safety of a fenced pasture and the secure but boring life of the fat livestock enclosed within. Stay in the game. Stay in the wilds. You will have reached a new level of personal awareness, and the Universe wants you to keep applying your keen mind as you travel onward. You are free and in control of your destiny. Your personal growth and increasing mental acuity are the consequences of your taking on the changes and challenges that life has given you.

The Four of Swords is also encouraging you to turn your thoughts inward like the four swords pointing at each other pictured on this card to fully understand and appreciate all that has brought you to this place. There will be more battles ahead, but you will carry forward with a medal of distinction for your personal courage and bravery. As always, do not let being overly ambitious steal these moments from you. Enjoy your rewards and advancements. There will be many challenges ahead, and you are well positioned to take them on successfully. Congratulations, honours, and accolades are in order!

Five of Swords

Viciousness - Stress - Chaos - Temper
Regret - Vexation - Anger - Turmoil

"Holding on to anger is like grasping a hot coal
with the intent of throwing it at someone else;
you are the one who gets burned."
- Buddha

When you draw the Five of Swords, you will soon be facing some serious obstacles and problems that will require all your mental strength. You will feel that you are under attack from more than one angle and that these attacks are personal. Whatever the conflicts are, your mind will be struggling to find solutions, and you will feel that you are near your wit's end. The word "wit" refers to your rational mind, and your rational mind, under constant attack like this, may be about to give up, hence the expression. Unfortunately, when your wit or rational mind gives up, your subconscious takes over. When this happens, you can lash out in irrational, dangerous, non-productive, and violent ways.

In most cases when this lashing out happens, you will regret your rash and dangerous actions. For example, you may have an adversarial supervisor who has pushed you into a state of extreme anger. You are so mad and angry! It is time to recall that the word "mad" also means "insane." While you are in this state of extreme anger and madness, you start shouting obscenities at your boss and then throw down your office keys as you stomp out of the room. The result is that you will not only lose your job but you will also have a bad reference follow you forward. This type of anger and action accomplishes nothing good other than making you feel better for a minute or two. It would be much healthier to channel your energy into rational, well-conceived plans and analytical, dispassionate confrontation. Another example may be seen in an escalated conflict between a parent and teenager. Once the yelling starts, both the parent and the teenager are likely to say things that they will regret later.

You should not let this situation that you will be facing hurt, ruin, or destroy you and your life. Your wit, or your rational mind, will be needed to get through these tough times. Take up the sword of decency, but do not take it up to cut down your opponents. Rather think of this sword as a beacon of your strength of will and your even greater trust in your mental ability to take charge and navigate through the situations that arrive. The high road is better choice. You are a grown-up. You can do this!

Six of Swords

Wellness - Acuity - Decisiveness - Certainty
Success - Partnerships - Engagement - Achievement

"We are all more capable than we think we are."
- Anne Murray

When you draw the Six of Swords, your intellect and mental fitness will soon be at full strength. All of your mental faculties will be working fine, and furthermore, you will have a very nice feeling of stability, as if there is a timelessness quality to your mind's sense of self and purpose. You will not have arrived at this place without a difficult and demanding journey. So now will be a good time to reflect on everything that has brought you to this wonderful state of mind. Further, if there is one particular person or force that has helped you, recognize and celebrate this force or person in your life. Also, use this time to reinforce your mental habits and abilities.

You will be called upon to help others make important decisions. In addition, you will be making clear-headed and significant decisions about your own life. These choices that you will be considering are not related to money or love; the options at this time will be related to life-style choices such as starting a new hobby or business. The choices that you will make can be life altering such as deciding to move to a new city or country. This card is telling you that you should not put off making any type of decision that will move you forward in your life. For example, something as simple as making a decision to join a choir, a gym, or yoga class can have far-reaching, positive consequences for you.

There are few feelings that are as wonderful as personal accomplishment. So, engage in some personal quest because you will be ready for it. For example, if you decide to lose weight and succeed, it is because you were ready for this decision and that moment when you see your new trim body in the mirror will be unlike any other. However, if you were not ready to lose weight and you did not follow through with your diet and exercise plans, you will feel even worse about yourself while staring into that same mirror. Thus, trust that you will have the resources, the strength of mind, and the necessary motivation to follow through with your decisions. Go for it! You are much stronger than you know. You will feel even stronger and more together as you move mindfully into your future. Look out world, here you come!

Seven of Swords

Frustration - Blockage - Irrationality - Anger
Irritation - Indignation - Resentment - Fury

"None but ourselves can free our minds."
- Bob Marley

When you draw the Seven of Swords, your mind will be soon be enduring a type of suspension and frustration with situations in your life that you want to go away, yet they stubbornly remain in place. Your thoughts will be confused or not fully formed, and as a result, your life will not be getting any place you need to be or should be. This will be a temporary situation that you will be able to solve with calm, rational thought and forward determination. Use your head above your heart. Your mind will be needed now to dispassionately assess, engage, and get over the obstructions stopping your forward progress and your greater satisfaction, happiness, and wellness.

This type of confusion and difficulty will breed frustration for you, and this frustration can result in wasted action at best or inaction at worst. For example, if you are unemployed and can see no opportunities out there because of the continual rejections of your applications, you may give up and stop looking for a job. You will remain bitter, broke, and broken. If you are employed but getting nowhere in your career, your frustration may cause you to engage in underground or open sabotage of your company and employer. All that you do while acting out your frustrations, such as gossiping or deliberately disrupting your workplace, will be wasted action and effort for your own life and career. This will accomplish nothing good.

Remember that you are in control and that all of this frustration will be temporary. Let your conscience and keen analytical mind supervene in your situation. As you do this, a big bonus will be all the important lessons that you will learn and for which you are ready. You can experience transcendental transformation through this conflict if you approach it in this manner. It still will be an unfortunate situation in which to find yourself, but do not make it worse than it is. Remember that you hold the big upright sword as pictured on this card. This sword is your rational and righteous mind. Behind you is the courage and determination needed to vanquish the puny and bent swords (also as pictured on this card) that will have surrounded you. Remember: no conflict, no story. So, start writing your story with you as the smart, savvy, and intelligent hero that you are.

Eight of Swords

Uncertainty - Fear - Confusion - Frustration
Despondency - Inaction - Obstruction - Difficulty

"Courage is being scared to death, but saddling up anyway."
- John Wayne

When you draw the Eight of Swords, your mind will
soon be overly focused on fear, confusion, and weakness.
There will be many conflicting thoughts troubling your
mind and also stopping other types of good, productive
thoughts. You will have to have to deal with your situation
because this is no way to live. It may be that your
subconscious is sensing danger ahead and keeps sending
your conscious mind various frightening prospects that you
sense more than you can clearly discern and deal with. This
will be causing you to be in a freeze mode, like the
defensive position of a possum or other animal that plays
dead to avoid predation. You will need to recall the adage
that rightly describes courage not as an absence of fear, but
rather as going forward in spite of fear.

For whatever reason, you will not be able to move
forward and get on with your life. All you may want to do is
hide, lay still, and hope it all goes away. You may be having
suicidal thoughts, thinking *wrongly* that death will *make*
everything go away. This, of course, is not the way onward
for you, and as such, you will need to break out of your
mental and physical immobility. The first order for you will

be to accept that your problems are not going to miraculously vanish. Next, will be to gather your courage and strength to make that all-important first step out of your situation. You will rediscover hope in yourself and your future as you select courage, bravery, valour, and gallantry over fear, escape, and disgrace.

As described above, you need to make a decision to step forward with resolution and action rather than succumbing to fear and inaction. Even something as simple as deciding to make your bed in the morning can have far-reaching consequences. Soldiers throughout history have had battle cries to spark their courage; for example, paratroopers in WWII would shout "GERONIMO!" as they left the plane. Appropriately, Geronimo was a brave Apache leader during the US Indian wars of the 1860s. You, too, will need a battle cry. Do not hang back, jump! GERONIMO!

Nine of Swords

Clarity - Purpose - Change - Strength
Transformation - Refocus - Happiness - Conversion

"There is only one way to happiness
and that is to cease worrying about things
that are beyond the power of your will."
- Epictetus

When you draw the Nine of Swords, much of your
current mental strife and stress will soon be ending. It will
appear to you that your psychological troubles are washing
away like dust in the rain. Those aspects of your life that
have been causing your mental anguish are not as they
seem. Be assured that the confusion and cloudiness that has
been reigning in your mind will soon be swept away to
reveal a much brighter and clear day. If you have started to
see the light after a dark period, expect and encourage this
change to continue. If you are still feeling the hopelessness
and darkness of despair and defeat, let this card give you
hope and light. The dark clouds in your mind will soon give
way to sunlight and clarity.

You need to stop stressing about problems that are
unsolvable, such as changing someone's personality.
Especially in this regard, you need to stop blaming yourself
for things beyond your control. This card reminds you that
you control your reactions to whatever is obscuring your
viewpoint. It might be just one annoying thing or person;
you cannot change this person or thing, but you can change

how you react and deal with this thing or person. For example, it may be as simple as accepting that your daughter wants to wear a nose ring if your reaction to this nose ring has been such that it clouds your view of your daughter and life in general.

You have your limits. You will feel much better once you reset your life with this in mind. Focus on what you can do and keep doing it. As you stop thinking and stressing about those things that are beyond your control, you will start moving forward again. If you feel yourself slipping back into darkness and despair, try to shake it off and leave it behind you. There will be a good road ahead for you and all of your talents. As the old saying goes, you cannot change your past, but you can create your future. The Nine of Swords assures you that you can part the curtains, look out on a sunny day, and start that glorious future today.

Ten of Swords

Heart-break - Loss - Anger - Frustration
Futility - Damage - Surrender - Learning

"The greatest glory lies not in never falling
but in rising each time we fall."
- Confucius

When you draw the Ten of Swords, you will be undergoing some serious mental difficulty. You will experience conflicting points of view and difficulty in making a compromise or a good choice. You will soon be thinking that you are unable to deal with the situation since there seems to be no positive way forward. Striking out, or lashing out at your situation will achieve nothing helpful at this time. It will end sooner when you surrender, let your heart break, and suffer. You will heal, and this predicament will take care of itself. But you will not get there by continuing to battle things, people, and situations that are unwinnable.

In times like these, it is best to let the Universe take care of you and your difficulties. Trust that those opposing forces that seem so harsh, unjustified, and cruel will get their karmic justice. This will help you to stop thinking and obsessing on them; it will also allow you to focus on yourself and your future. There is always something to learn from situations like these, and as soon as you learn your lesson and advance your soul, things will start looking much better for you. Essentially, the less time you spend worried, angry, frustrated, vindictive, and thirsty for revenge, the better it will be for you.

Behind the confusion, frustration, anger, and broken-heart of the present, there will be a wonderful world waiting for you in the distance. This card is telling you to take a step back, lay down your weapons, regroup, and heal your wounds. You will find a way to quiet the noise and conflict in your head, and this will help nurture, heal, and advance your life. As you realize that you cannot change others, you will step out of your struggles. Also as you forgive, forget, and move on, your life will suddenly start looking much better. As bonus, you will learn some key lessons which will help to make your life even better than it was before this happened to you.

Princess of Swords

Strength - Certainty - Battle - Justice
Energy - Victory - Honour - Reputation

"The world is not always the most pleasant place.
You need to learn to stand up for yourself
and what you believe in
and, pardon my language, kick some ass."
- Queen Elizabeth II

When you draw the Princess of Swords, you will soon
need to stand up for yourself and your ideas. As you do this,
you will feel strong, courageous, and confident, and in this
state of mind, you will both overcome your opposition and
reaffirm your goodness and righteousness. You may be in a
position where someone is about to metaphorically stab you
in the back. There may be some point of personal honour
that you will be called on to defend. Whatever happens, you
will prevail when you act on behalf of honour and justice.

This card is telling you to keep to the higher ground and
to not give an inch to lower yourself. As you engage your
youthful ideals and clear-headed conceptions of right and
wrong, your honour and principles will not be forsaken for
the lies, deceit, dishonour that are about to threaten your
reputation. Also, look closely at the princess pictured on this
card: she is nimble and light, ready to make quick decisions
even if they turn out to be mistakes. She is unafraid and
ready to do what she must do and what she knows she must
do. For example, if someone is spreading lies about her, she

would not do the same to that person as in an eye-for-eye revenge. She would confront that person directly, immediately. She would not indulge in long, drawn-out battles with ignorant and destructive people who are threatening her. She would act quickly, almost instinctually, to defend herself and her ideals. This will be the best course of action for you as well.

It will be a time for you to trust your regal ideals, energy, and power. Never think that you are weak because you are *not* weak. You are incredibly strong in anything that matters. Never deny your enthusiastic passion and power to protect yourself by being light, nimble, and deadly in the face of weighty old adversaries who tempt you to forsake your honour and principles. You will be victorious if you follow this card's advice, and although your life is good right now, it will get even better. Go ahead, like Queen Elizabeth says, "Kick some ass!"

Prince of Swords

Boldness - Certainty - Courage - Competition
Victory - Advancement - Acuity - Precision

"Whatever you do or dream you can, begin it.
Boldness has genius, power, and magic in it.
- Goethe

When you draw the Prince of Swords, you will soon be charging forward into a situation and part of your life that will require your mental strength and energy. But you will be more than ready for this, and as such, your success is assured. You will feel powerful, confident, and victorious. Consider that you are soon to be entering a new land as a strong, wise, and potentially legendary prince. You may be starting a new job, a new school, a new relationship, a new life (children), or some other new and significant aspect of your life. You will not have to wait around for things to happen and for your move forward. These changes will strike like lightning. You will feel mentally strong, fit, exhilarated, and certain that you are on the right path in your life as this happens.

As mentioned, you will soon be entering some new phase of your life that will call upon your mental strength and certainty. Whatever this new phase may be, the outcomes look very favourable as long as doubts and insecurities fade far into the background. As an old saying goes, fortune favours the bold, and this will be good mantra for you as you move forward. This card is encouraging you to go forward boldly and not be afraid to take on new and difficult challenges. What good is a strong and capable mind if it is never put to use or never put to the test? A sword will get dull if it is not used and sharpened and so will your mind.

This card is encouraging you to engage your competitive nature to get ahead and overcome your enemies, whether they be internal doubts and fears or external forces that hold you back. You will best be served if you model the warrior prince pictured on this card using your rational, logical, and serious mind. When you remain principled and tough, rather than sentimental and sympathetic, you will be able to travel forward with youthful, positive energy as you enter this new phase of your life. Straighten up that strong backbone of yours. Grab your great golden sword as pictured on this card. This sword is an apt representation of your mind and its shining intensity and power. Move forward. Look out world, here you come!

Queen of Swords

Virtue - Honour - Victory - Conviction
Righteousness - Dignity - Passion - Honesty

"All battles are first won or lost in the mind.
- Joan of Arc

When you draw the Queen of Swords, your mind will soon be in a very good and powerful place. You will soon be clearly victorious in your life, overcoming some significant obstacle and advancing triumphantly through conflict and opposition. You will feel strong, empowered, and on the right side of honour, justice, and principle. This will be a time for you to be proud, strong, and passionate about your values, abilities, and regal nature. You may have to subdue some of your rationality and logic to fully engage your instincts and your overpowering conviction. Your mind should be the image of a strong, commanding queen who is fearlessly defending her home and family. Is there anything more unstoppable than that?

You will have to confront lies and deceit. When this happens, stand your ground and do not give up your ideals, purpose, and honour. Listen to and trust your conscience and your innate sense of right and wrong. It may be that someone will be telling you lies such as an unfaithful partner, or perhaps a family member or friend will be trying to get you to buy into some get-rich-quick scam. It may be that someone will be trying to get you to do things that you do not want to do and know are wrong. Recall how easily your mind can equivocate and convince you that even the most horrible things are necessary and justified. There are many reasons to do any number of things that your conscience says that you should not do.

As you go forward, you must metaphorically cut off the heads of those forces or people who are trying to justify their lies, deceit, and immoral actions. This metaphor is clearly illustrated in this card's imagery. The Queen of Swords holds a severed head in one hand and a sword in her other hand. Like this victorious queen, you will need to make a clean, effective, and decisive cut with your sword and mind. Do not even listen to their arguments. You have the silver sword of truth in your hands: use it. Do not let yourself believe the deceivers and charlatans. You are so much better than that. And your life will be so much better once you have metaphorically beheaded those equivocators and liars. It will be glorious! It will be wonderful and the right thing to do. Stand up proud, certain, victorious, truthful, beautiful, and righteous. Nothing can stop the virtuous queen when she takes on her corrupt enemies at home or abroad in the wide world.

Knight of Swords

Conviction - Defense - Conquest - Strength
Struggle - Growth - Empowerment - Triumph

"There's a worthy and noble ambition:
strength in the face of adversity. That is very different
from the wish for a life free of trouble."
- Jordan B. Peterson

When you draw the Knight of Swords, your mind will soon be in a wonderfully powerful and victorious place. When you are called upon to defend your home, yourself, your family, or friends, you will have the ability to overpower all threats and enemies whatever or whomever they may be. As can be seen in this card's metaphoric imagery, it is time to mount your great steed, brandish your weapons in both hands, one short sword for close threats and one long sword for those further away. Your mind will be in a magnificent place, and you are sure to enjoy yourself. Life without conflicts is no life at all. Struggle brings strength, happiness, and personal growth. Trust in your instincts of conquest and glory; subdue your tenderness, and be like a battle-hardened knight protecting his castle. Trust your incredible, unyielding conviction, strength, and power.

You have amassed your honour, position, and might through many battles and confrontations that are part of the Knights' quest and journey. As such, you should feel confident and well prepared to sweep away whatever is trying to pull you, and others around you, down. Be battle-ready! Be confident and poised. Conflicts and threats never cease in the human condition. There are, of course, times when they are far away, and you can focus on other things that peace will bring to you. However, this will not one of those times. Nevertheless, be assured that in your near future, you will triumph over these dangers and struggles as long as you do not let go of your convictions, ideals, courage, and bravery.

It may be that someone is attempting to upset you and your close circle of family and friends, and this person needs to be told to leave. It may be that some negative person from your past is again trying to enter your life and bring you down. It may be that someone is spreading lies about you. Whatever this attack may be, do not be afraid to act quickly, confidently, and decisively to defend your knightly and personal honour. You are in a great place. You have the strength, conviction, resources, and experience to rise to all challenges. Charge forward! Your enemies will scatter like sparrows when they see a hawk.

Pentacles

"Money and success do not change people;
they only amplify what is already there."
- Will Smith

The fifth card that you will draw will be from the suit of Pentacles. Shuffle the Pentacles and lay down the card in the final position of the five-pointed star pattern that your cards have created. This will be in the bottom left, below your Cups card and beside your Wands card.

The Pentacles suit represents the element earth. This is the element that pertains to things such as money and other material things in your life. In some traditions, the Pentacles are referred to as coins to make this connection more explicit. It also makes sense that this is the final card in your spread because everything eventually comes back to the earth.

Some Tarot decks purposely avoid using the pentacle for this suit because of all the other magical properties and lore associated with the five-pointed star. However, when the pentacle *is* used for this suit, as is the case with the Millennium Thoth Tarot, you have to consider the elemental meaning of the suit above these other associations.

Nevertheless, you *can* embrace all the meanings and lore that is associated with the pentacle as you engage in the five-card pentacle layout and reading. This is to say that as you complete your five-card reading from the Tarot and you see the pentacle shape that your cards have made, you can assure yourself that your card layout carries with it all the good vibrations, protective energy, and positive fortune associated with this ancient symbol.

The Tarot should never be used for negative purposes such as to find ways to get even with others or any other type of selfish, devious, or destructive desires. Clear your mind of all negativity, anger, and selfishness when engaging with the cards. Always treat the cards with the greatest respect and do not engage with them until you feel ready.

It is good practice to say a little prayer of thanks before shuffling any of the suits, but perhaps even more so with the Pentacles. Simply, give thanks for all the material blessings in your life as you would give thanks for all the spiritual, emotional, intellectual blessings that correspond to the other suits.

As you shuffle the Pentacles, ask the Universe to provide you with advice and knowledge about your earthly needs. You can meditate on your financial situation, such as wondering if you should invest in a new car. However, do not ask for material blessings as if the Tarot is a type of Santa Claus. Rather, ask for guidance and in how to best carry forward in your life.

Divine spirit of Earth, please send me advice on how best to conduct my earthly affairs for prosperity, happiness, and abundance. Glorious Universe, direct me in how I may best use my resources to advance my journey and quest for the betterment of myself and others.

Ace of Pentacles

Newness - Commitment - Fortune - Blessing
Wellness - Abundance - Growth - Happiness

"Be yourself; everyone else is already taken."
- Charles M. Shultz

When you draw the Ace of Pentacles, you will soon be starting something that will end well for you and your material benefit. This will be a time to plant seeds (real or metaphoric) and tend to them. In particular, this will be a good time to reflect on what single thing you would like to achieve in your life and dive into it with energy and enthusiasm. Feel the power of certainty as you step forward. This will be especially important for you if you have been somewhat hesitant to get going on a new project or other potentially profitable changes in your life.

Your wellness and good fortune matter. These things are tied into your identity. This card is encouraging you to engage in the things that enhance your identity. For example, if you identify as a guitar player, you should be playing more guitar. If you identify as a writer, you should be writing more. This is not to say that your life will become easier, but easier does not always mean better. You will have your share of struggle and discord, contrary to the wrong-headed belief that the absence of conflict equals happiness. Nevertheless, your life will not be all tussle and trouble when you step forward gracefully, gratefully, and gainfully. Keep working; stay active and productive and good fortune will follow.

You have your own life to live, and your life is not a competition. Accept and nurture your own unique relationship with the Universe and *your* life. If you have a tendency towards procrastination, and you have been delaying starting that labour of love that will manifest your destiny, this card is saying start *now*! As Lao Tzu once said, "A journey of a thousand miles begins with a single step." You will soon be on your way. Go forward on a wonderful journey and quest that is bound to bring you many good things. Step one. Step two. Keep going.

Two of Pentacles

Balance - Contentment - Productivity - Wellness
Wealth - Goodness - Satisfaction - Health

"Step with care and great tact. And remember
life's a great balancing act."
- Dr. Seuss

When you draw the Two of Pentacles, you will soon strike a productive balance between two conflicting or opposing elements in your life. This balance between opposites will lead you to increased material wellness, good fortune, and dynamic personal growth. It will be a time to end the struggle, accept the outcome, and carry on much better off than you were previously. Keep in mind that this new peaceful and productive balance will *not* enter your life without your involvement. You will need to make some changes in order for this beneficial balance to happen. It will not be easy, and these choices will be life-style, long-term choices. But the results will be well worth it.

Balance is a primary feature of all well-lived lives. This card is telling you to take time to examine your life and ask yourself if some parts of your life are out of balance with each other. On a basic level, this involves questions like are you getting enough sleep, exercise, food, recreation? Or are you getting *too much* sleep, exercise, food, recreation? On a deeper level, this involves the balance between your heart and your head. For example, are you being too emotional or are you being too rational? Another potential imbalance is the one between your wealth and your health. For example, are you trading your health for wealth by working too hard? Too much of anything is not good. Good fortune, health, and contentment will be yours as you adjust your life accordingly to achieve that sweet equilibrium.

This card is not pointing at anything in particular; it is here to remind you and encourage you to make necessary changes that will bring not only balance into your life but also all the wonderful benefits that follow from this balance. Consider that if you are happy going to work in the morning and happy coming home in the evening, you are rich! So find that happy balance and enjoy all the various paybacks that come from that beautiful, stable, secure place in the Universe. Step forward and create that life that is only a few important, long-term changes away from being yours. Carry forward in your journey and quest as a balanced person. Life *is* a balancing act and that is part of life's wondrous beauty and continuing challenge.

Three of Pentacles

Prosperity - Comfort - Balance - Satisfaction
Happiness - Completeness - Reward - Profit

"Heaven has given humanity three things to balance
the odds of life: Hope, sleep, and laughter."
- Immanuel Kant

When you draw the Three of Pentacles, you will soon be working toward something that will bring your life many material benefits. This prosperity will involve cooperation and collaboration with two other people. It will also involve your balancing three aspects of your life in an ideal and productive manner. For example, if you have been overly focused and obsessed with one thing, it is time to break away from that tyranny. Alternatively, if you have been trying to do too many things at once, it is time to refocus your life on a much smaller number of objectives and activities.

Consider the concept of triangulation and the power of three. The triangle is the most stable of all geometric forms with its angles always adding up to a perfect 180 and each side supporting the other two sides. In research, triangulation means finding three sources to support a thesis. Three mutually supporting particles (electrons, protons, neutrons) make up all known matter. This is not a coincidence. And it is not a coincidence that you have drawn this card. This card is here to encourage you to use the magic and power of three. Either increase or decrease

your life's key components and people to make that
charmed number.

   As you proceed, examine your life by considering how the
power of three is, or is not, working for you. There is
always a danger for you to become too specialized and too
narrowly defined. There is also always a danger for you to
become too scattered and unfocused. The power of three
will provide you balance, prosperity, and enrichment. You
are in a good place, and you have the resources available to
you. Continue to be strong, stable, and structured. Do not
become too singular. Do not become too plural. Become
triangular! These foundations will support you well in all
that you do.

Four of Pentacles

Prosperity - Stability - Consistency - Growth
Influence - Gain - Security - Advance

"Do good and good will come to you."
- Ukrainian Proverb

When you draw the Four of Pentacles, you will soon be acquiring the material resources that you need for stability, prosperity, and security. Your efforts in building good things with strong and stable foundations will bring you many blessings. This refers to your family, your career, your home, and your bank account. Warning: do not spoil this goodness by falling into the depressing trap of contrasting your material wealth with the material wealth of others. Focus on your own life and giving it your best. Finally, this card is telling you to stay conservative: it is not a time for taking unnecessary financial risks.

As mentioned above, you will be seeing many benefits coming into your life in the near future. However, these rewards will be of the real kind for which you have worked. For example, if you have had an exercise routine to which you have adhered, the rewards may not be evident in the first few weeks, but after a few months of doing your routine, you will start to see your new body emerging from the older one. Likewise, with many other things, it takes time and effort to build the castle of your life, brick by brick. Keep on working, doing the right things, and do not forget to smile. Be grateful and generous with your good fortune. Enjoy the process, including the difficulties and struggles, more than the final product.

When you do things that matter, you will feel good. You will feel the power and blessings that come from hard and honest work. Consider how quickly a house or car will fall apart if they are not regularly maintained, cleaned, and loved. Consider also how good you feel driving in your newly-cleaned car versus how you feel in in a messy, smelly, and dirty car. If you treasure what you have and are prepare to treasure the blessings coming your way, your future looks wonderful! As you continue to maintain and enhance your good habits, especially as they relate to health, work, and money, you will continue to be in a good place. As you keep going forward with honesty, goodwill, and diligence, your life will get even better! Keep on building, one brick at a time.

Five of Pentacles

Failure - Harm - Breakdown - Loss
Impairment - Destruction - Endings - Closure

"Never let success go to your head
or failure go to your heart."
- North American Proverb

When you draw the Five of Pentacles, you will soon be experiencing a catastrophic interruption that will bring your forward material progress to a standstill. Keep in mind that this may not be a bad thing. It happens all the time. Not everything that you put together and put your energies into works out for you. When this happens, the best thing to do is to move on. The sooner that you leave the wreckage behind, live and learn, the better it will be for you; in addition, this will ensure that this misfortune does not set you back permanently.

There is, as with everything, a purpose behind whatever happens to you. As you look for the bright side, and do not let this potential disaster go to your heart or your head, this calamity will not take more from your life than it should. One of the things that separates highly successful people from others is how they handle failure. Conrad Hilton, of the famous hotel chain that bears his name says, "Successful people make mistakes, but they do not quit." You can find this self-help advice and encouragement from nearly every successful person because nearly every successful person has gone through at least one disastrous time and situation like the one that you will be facing and must get through.

The thing to remember about all these successful people is that they did not quit when this card came up in their lives. They kept going. Perhaps this card will be a forewarning for you. As such, you may be able to lessen the damage by making necessary changes now. For example, if you have a business partnership that is falling apart, but you are stubbornly holding on to it, consider getting out of this partnership sooner rather than later. Thus, you will minimize your losses. Although it is easy to give this advice, it is not so easy to accept it. Remind yourself of what Nelson Mandela said, "I never lose; I either win or I learn." All will be well, in time, if you follow this advice and keep your heart and head strong. It is okay to be sad; it is not okay to give up. *Never* give up!

Six of Pentacles

Success - Advancement - Teamwork - Cooperation
Moderation - Conservatism - Stability - Security

"Excellence is not a gift, but a skill that takes practice."
- Plato

When you draw the Six of Pentacles, you will soon be experiencing material success and advancement. This will be the result of resolving some significant conflicts or solving some serious problems that have been plaguing your life. This resolution or solution will bring you good fortune, wealth, and wellness. You should carry forward with your choices and direction. You are on the right road, and while this card does not point to riches dropping out of nowhere, such as winning the lottery, this card is telling you to continue forward with cooperation, moderation, and stability. There will be room for improvement; therefore, keep practicing excellence. You can make a wish upon a star, but also wish for the strength to keep following your dreams as you have been doing.

You will be in a good place, and you should be able to continue advancing with caution and practicality. You know that this kind of success does not happen on its own. You have to make many constructive choices, and you have to endure your share of work and hardship to get to this place. But this is the most valuable thing of all. When people are given riches and position that they did not work for, they usually do not appreciate the money or status. The net result for them is bitterness and unhappiness. This is *not* your destiny!

You will need to keep on working to maintain this place, but you will not have to work as hard or as strenuously. You can work from this position of strength with better focus and joy aiming to manifest your destiny as your future unfolds. Keep close to those people who are helping you forward on your journey. Share your wealth and success; your kindness and generosity will bring you even more goodness and profit. The Six of Pentacles is about moderation in all things as you travel onward. Keep on going. Bring it on! You and your team are ready for it. Enjoy, share, be grateful. Continue to plant, nurture, and harvest all the wonders of this wonderful planet that you share, care for, and bring to fruition.

Seven of Pentacles

Loss - Trouble - Damage - Self-pity
Failure - Disappointment - Harm - Pain

"Feeling sorry for yourself and your present
condition is not only a waste of energy,
it is the worst habit you could possibly have."
- Dale Carnegie

When you draw the Seven of Pentacles, you will soon be having some serious material disappointments and failures. If you make some changes, you can lessen these unfortunate consequences. The first change can be your attitude. For example, if you indulge in pessimism, failure, and self-pity, things will only get worse. These kinds of self-defeating thoughts will strangle you and your future as is suggested in the visual imagery on this card. Aside from your attitude, you can also halt whatever will be bringing you this potential financial ruin if you are able foresee or sense where things are going wrong in your financial life and make some changes today.

There will be failure and disappointment in your life, and this card is letting you know that, unfortunately, you will be experiencing some of this in your near future. How you deal this failure and disappointment will be what counts. You will get over this hump in the road if you keep going forward. You will have to stop waiting to win the lottery and start making some positive changes in your material life. As you leave behind what is not working and focus on what is working for you and as lose your gloomy, self-pitying, and pessimistic outlook, you will minimize your losses and the time spent in this place. You still have your freedom, and you can focus on all the opportunities, challenges, and future golden days ahead of you!

This predicament cannot stop your forward progress indefinitely. As Zig Ziglar has said, "Other people and things can stop you temporarily, but you are the only one who can do it permanently." You are always a lot stronger than you think you are, and this is not where you are meant to be. If you keep moving, you will move out of this dark, strangling, and death-like place. You will find your way and come out stronger, wiser, and ready to engage in life and experience success again. It is up to you. It is *not* a lottery win that will give you your release. Start today. Get moving! Keep moving.

Eight of Pentacles

Reward - Effort - Success - Harvest
Consistency - Advancement - Achievement - Prize

"If you are too lazy to plough,
then you should never expect a harvest."
- Proverbs, 20:4

When you draw the Eight of Pentacles, you will soon be in a fortunate and happy position. You will be growing, tending, and harvesting a bounty of good things in your life. You will enjoy the rewards that will have come from your dedicated, cooperative, and consistent effort. It has not been easy for you to get to this place. Your environment has been harsh and demanding. Nevertheless, your diligence and persistence has endured, and things are about to become somewhat easier for you. You will be in a position to gather some of the abundance that you have worked so hard to attain. Your future looks good, stable, and profitable.

Remind yourself of the things that matter in generating material success. Of these things, hope is the most important. Next comes determination. This is followed by gratitude. Finally, there is the consistently applied effort of getting up in the morning and going to work. Nevertheless, it is also good to recall that your efforts do not *always* guarantee success. As such, do not forget to be grateful for the good fortune that has followed you to this place. There is always an element of chance or luck at play in your life, and this applies even now when you are being more directly rewarded for your hard work.

Continue to cultivate your strong roots and values that have brought you this far. Also, keep your circle of supportive friends and family close to you. Maintain your discipline and conservative outlook and habits. Life is good and will get even better. You are on a good path toward material wellness and all the other benefits that come from wealth and security. Your rewards will be even more valuable and appreciated, the harder you have had to work for them. So do not lose your work ethic. That may be the most important thing that you possess. Keep hope, optimism, and gratefulness flowing through you. Now get back to work!

Nine of Pentacles

Wellness - Success - Charity - Kindness
Happiness - Attainment - Sharing - Plenty

"The highest compliment that you can pay me is
to say that I work hard every day, that I never dog it."
- Wayne Gretzky

When you draw the Nine of Pentacles, you will be blessed with good fortune, success, and wealth. These blessings will extend into other aspects of your life, such as your health and happiness. You will feel these blessings radiate outward from you in all directions, and you will be helping others, especially those close to you. This card is saying that you soon will be living a life that you are meant to live. Your efforts will be bringing rewards, and it may feel that "money is dropping into your lap" as an old saying goes. Therefore, you should continue whatever it is you are doing.

Be careful not to get overconfident with your success wrongly thinking that this prosperous state will continue without your continued effort and focus. Also do not become extravagant with your success and wealth. Stay conservative. Finally, do not become greedy or overly ambitious. Greed and excessive ambition will bring you down from this place. Stay in this zone as long as you can by being grateful, happy, generous, kind, humble, and hardworking.

This card is also encouraging you to listen to and consider all types of people and related viewpoints. Ultimately, you will be the one to make the decisions that will affect your life and lead to your success, but your decisions will be better if you keep seeking advice and wisdom from others. Also, your success will be much more enjoyable if you do not become arrogant or bullyish. As you stay balanced, fair, and generous as well as continue cultivating friendly relationships with all of those who surround you and are part of your success, you will be assured of more material blessings and success. Let this card be your reinforcer and shining light for your added confidence and strength to avoid temptations and wrong-way paths that are bound to cross your forward journey. You *can* lose, but you will not lose if you keep that thought in your head. Onward with wisdom, grace, and good fortune!

Ten of Pentacles

Success - Happiness - Zenith - Comfort
Blessings - Attainment - Riches - Goodness

"If you get up in the morning and think that the future is
going to be better, then it is a bright day."
- Elon Musk

When you draw the Ten of Pentacles, you will soon be blessed with an abundance of resources and opportunities. In fact, this card is telling you that your life will soon be at a place where it cannot get any better than it will be. You will soon be completing some successful project or venture. Your hard work will pay off handsomely. You will be rewarded with more opportunities. But, be prepared for a plateau of sorts. It will be a glorious plateau, so enjoy it. Avoiding all excesses and moral temptations that are bound to be so much more accessible and available to you in your near future will keep you in this wonderful place longer than if you fall for these snares of success.

Do not make the mistake of overly ambitious people who reach these levels but then spot something or some position that still eludes their grasp. Their joy in their success is, thus, very short-lived, and their obsessive ambition can and usually does lead to serious personal tragedies. So make sure to take time to enjoy your success and achievement. Ironically, the more your share your fortune and success with others, the more good fortune and success will come your way. As you remain humble, grateful, and generous, you will gain respect, admiration, and approval.

Although you have played a part in getting to where you are, fortune has played an equal part. This is why it is so important for you to never get too high on yourself when success comes your way or too low on yourself when failure befalls you. This card wants you to stay unpretentious and reserved; there will be plenty of time for more trials and struggles, so let this time of success be a bedrock that you will build on and never fall below. Congratulations! You will not be able to stay at this wonderful level forever, and neither do you want to. There is so much more that you can accomplish, more mountains to climb, more life to live.

Princess of Pentacles

Compassion - Protection - Opportunity - Advancement
Strength - Attraction - Creativity - Delight

"The magic is inside you; there ain't no crystal ball."
- Dolly Parton

When you draw the Princess of Pentacles, you will soon be enjoying many earthly blessings, but you will need to stand firm and protect them from those who would use you or otherwise take from you. Be assured that you will be strong and capable of defending yourself. You will deflect and defeat these destructive forces, and you will use your attraction, charm, and personal warmth to move yourself forward.

There will also be many backdoors opening for you at this time. Your personal connections with others and your ability to draw people to you, will provide you with more opportunities than you will get from traditional resume submissions, for example. You will be irresistible, and as such, many people will want to bring you into their circle. Also, your creative powers will be at a high point. You should manifest these to further your earthly blessings. Engage or continue your creativity and creative pursuits. Things will be falling into place for you. If you use this time wisely, the gains and relationships that you make will serve you long into your future.

Be careful, however, that you are not seduced by those who want to use you. You will need to be especially wary of powerful, greedy people. Due to your strong attractive power, these negative and potentially-destructive people will be anxious to be around you, so beware and trust your intuition. When you hear the con artists and charlatans out there, politely withdraw. This card is encouraging you to be patient, kind, and compassionate. You will be in an extraordinary place. Great things will happen to you. You will also be able to do wonderful things for others, especially the weak and suffering who will benefit greatly from your compassion and assistance. Stay the course. Enjoy the ride. Smile and bring it on!

Prince of Pentacles

Steadiness - Progress - Happiness - Accumulation
Protection - Command - Influence - Goodness

"You don't win by being good. You win with hard work
and sacrifice. Without that, skill is just potential."
- Bobby Orr

When you draw the Prince of Pentacles, you will soon be
in a place of abundance, prosperity, and general wellness.
This card is encouraging you to keep moving steadily
forward in your life with a clear purpose and direction.
There will be no need for you to rush. You have come a
considerable way, but you will have more to go. Your
fortune will continue to grow as you keep planting and
tending the seeds that will grow into many benefits in your
life and in the lives of others.

This card is also telling you to be cautious and
conservative, not rash and impetuous, as you travel forward.
In addition, you will need to avoid any princely conceit and
related arrogance that may be entering your mind. A good
prince has to work twice as hard at being nice than a regular
person because so many people will be jealous of your
princely nature and your assumed privilege. You will be
best served if you treasure all that you have and carry with
you. If you start taking things for granted and become
careless and pleasure-seeking, your fortune will not last
long. Finally, as the Prince of Pentacles, you should not
engage in too much tenderness or become overly generous

with your fortune. Carry on with strength, purpose, and conviction.

As pictured in this card, having a good, hard-working ox pulling your cart forward is far more practical and beneficial for you than having a showy and headstrong thoroughbred. While an ox can never outrun a horse, it can outwork and outlast a horse. Consider this as you move steadily forward. If you keep focused on the road ahead, your possessions, and your higher aims, you will be rewarded richly for your efforts, and your long-term prospects look very good, especially if you continue with your conservative, yet productive, tendencies. Be careful, competent, and firm. You are awesome! Take aim on your glorious future and roll on!

Queen of Pentacles

Influence - Generosity - Wisdom - Success
Wealth - Affluence - Stability - Kindness

"Leave every place you go, everything you touch,
a little better for your having been there."
- Julie Andrews

When you draw the Queen of Pentacles, you will soon be having much wealth and good fortune. You will soon be in a place of comfort and influence. This card is gently reminding you to hold onto your position and wealth, but not in a greedy or needy way. Further, this card is encouraging you to be generous. But, being generous does not mean giving away your fortune. Your future will be best served by using your wealth, influence, and position to help those who appeal to your nurturing and kind spirit. For example, your kindness to animals may extend to the giving some of your time or money to a cause like the SPCA. Whatever you do, everything will work out for you as you stay noble, royal, and use your reputable intellect in all things.

You will need to consider how you can do wonderful and helpful things without overextending yourself. You have not arrived at such a powerful and noble position to burnout in short-term projects. As you do this, it will be best to not give too much of yourself. When you conserve your energy and keep plenty of your passion in reserve, you will be aligning well with what this card represents for you. Also, when deciding your path forward, it will be best for you to trust your own wisdom and intuition rather than seeking advice from others. Your sense of propriety and rightness will be very keen and does not need opposing viewpoints to muddy it. Stick to your convictions and your instincts. These instincts will be those that lean toward compassion and empathy. Use your heart, feel the implications of your actions, but stay queenly, and do what must be done.

This card is reminding you to take a calm and reasonable view of things. As you remain stately and honourable in your manners, aspects, and resources, you will eliminate any neurotic worries and potentially bad habits. You will be confident and strong. As you accept that with your position and status come certain responsibilities, you will continue to rise above the ordinary and never lose your good fortune. You will be a shining example of a good Queen, holding much in reserve and spreading goodwill, kindness, and happiness everywhere you go. People will look up to you. You will be valued and respected. Live the dream! Be the dream!

Knight of Pentacles

Goodness - Strength - Character - Wealth
Reward - Protection - Triumph - Firmness.

"It is not in the stars to hold our destiny; it is in ourselves."
- William Shakespeare

When you draw the Knight of Pentacles, you will soon be in a wonderful position of material wellness, confidence, authority, and influence. Your material life cannot get much better than it will soon become. Everything will be coming together for you, and you will feel strong, full of energy, with plenty of reserves to maintain this position into the foreseeable future. Whatever it is that you have been doing and are soon to be embarking upon should be continued. You should try to stay in this magnificent position and phase for as long as possible. Take on all enemies! Life is good, and this card is reaffirming your direction, character, habits, confidence, and strength.

This will be a good time to look forward into your future. What challenges do you see for yourself and your life? As a rule, you should not shy away from these challenges because you will be so well positioned to succeed at these missions and opportunities. This card wants you to become the virtuous, honorable, and enduring Knight who is rarely, if ever, impetuous, bad-tempered, or worst of all, injudicious or careless. Also, this card affirms that you will *not* be ready to retire to the rocking chair any time soon. Why should you? You have worked hard to get where you are and as the old saying goes, "It is not the destination that matters—it is the journey!" Consider the virtues and effectiveness of protective strength, forceful advancement, personal freedom, and other hard-hitting techniques of the champion Knight as you move forward. These will serve you well now and far into your future.

This card is also encouraging you to keep your eyes on the big canvas of life rather than on the small details that can bog or slow you down. In addition, it will *not* be the time to lay down your weapons, shields, and armour. You may have need of these, and besides, these accoutrements of yours are well worn and fit you to perfection as is pictured on this card. Keep on going forward. You will be strong. You will be on the right path. You will have more battles and likely an equal number of victories ahead of you. Travel on! Life is good! It is good to be you.

Afterword

Writing this book on the Tarot and the Five-Card Pentacle Layout has been wonderful. It also has reaffirmed my belief in the magic and utility of the Tarot cards themselves. The cards are an amazing legacy that has been passed down through the history of our known humanity. They represent a range of the human condition that is remarkable in its clarity, purpose, depth, and iconography.

My resolution has been to add something to the lore and legacy of the Tarot using the Millennial Thoth deck. The Millennial Thoth is a new Tarot deck having been released within the past three years. I believe that it will be an enduring deck, and if this book helps in this regard, I will be pleased.

I would like to thank Renata Lechner who created the Millennium Thoth Tarot. I find continual inspiration in the wonderful artwork and metaphysical vibration that she has put in each card. Without her artwork, this book would not have been written.

I also want to thank her publisher, Lo Scarabeo, who has published and distributed this magnificent deck across the world. In addition, my gratitude is extended to her publisher for allowing me to use the beautiful images from the Trump cards.

My gratitude extends to my editor and daughter, Alison Lund. She has provided invaluable advice and editorial content for this book and designed the magical cover art. My sincere thanks as well to my daughter, Emily Machura, for her important contributions to this publication. My love to them both for their commitment and help. Finally, thanks and love to my life-partner, Brenda Fraser, who also provided crucial advice and encouragement as this book was being written and finally published.

Lastly, I am grateful to the Universe for giving me this opportunity and means to carry on in this time and space. If my book brings you into a closer relationship with the Universe, I will be glad.

Strive for harmony, listen to your conscience, and listen to the music of the stars. Your life matters and nothing is more important than your spirit. Nurture it, love it, and share your life others and the Universe itself. You are not meant to live alone.

Act as if everything you do and say matters: it does. Above all, love yourself and your precious time on this beautiful blue planet that is your home. You are special, unique, loved, wanted, and needed. Travel on!

- Marv Machura

About the Author

Marv Machura is a writer, teacher, and performer. He, like many other musicians, has psychic abilities that he has practiced over his lifetime. His grandfather first opened the world of psychic vibrations by showing him how to find underground water by channeling the vibrations with a willow branch. Machura realized that he could see into the regular card deck at a young age and practiced this for many years with friends and family. He moved on to the Tarot deck when he started practicing as a professional psychic at farmers' markets and events around his hometown of Vernon, BC. As a student-centred classroom teacher, he has taught and transformed the lives of many thousands of students over his 35+ year career. He has also presented many conferences and published many articles on teaching and learning, Marshal McLuhan media ecology, and the transcendental, transformational nature of classroom experience. As a singer-songwriter, he has released four CDs and many singles and continues to write, record, produce, and perform music. He is known as a neo-folk artist of Western Canada. He is also an engaging live performer who continues to perform at events, festivals, and concerts. He has performed for many thousands of people over his 40+ years as a professional singer, guitarist, and band leader. As a writer, Machura has published many articles, poems, and stories. He recently published a collection of poetry, *Wonder*, which explores those moments of miracle, transformation, and clarity that come to us when we see into the infinite. He currently lives in Vernon, British Columbia with his life-partner, Brenda Fraser, their cat, Nahatik, and their dog, Cherie Amour. Visit marvmachura.com for more information and to get in touch with the author.

Rapture

Like the early-spring crocus flowers,
That push half-frozen grains of soil aside,
And overturn the tiny clods to leaf and blossom,
My awakening to beauty lifts
Mounds of mortality in me.

My regular breath
Changes suddenly
As something
From inside rises
And up-ends those clods
From which I am made.

I know this rapture is infused by my senses
But there is more:
As if inside this dusty container
There is a seed
That rumbles,
Wanting to shed its shell and reach
Upward and outward regardless of explanation
Making imperfect sense,
For that all-important moment of truth,
Beauty, and wonder.

- Marv Machura,
from *Wonder, A Collection of Poems* (2012)